The Global Currency Plot

The Mises Institute dedicates this volume to all of its generous Supporters and wishes to thank these, in particular:

Patrons

Abdelhamid Abdou
Mr. and Mrs. J. Ryan Alford
Dr. Thomas T. Amlie
Mr. and Mrs. Michael Asselta
Jordan Ausman
Shawn Bardong
Bryan Lee Briggs
Michael L. Burks
Travis Coursey
Richard Cunniff
Jerry T. Dowell
Gerald Dungee, in Memory of Paul S. Dungee
Bill Eaton
Dennis Edwards
Julian Fondren
Lee Friday
Charles F. Hanes
Mr. and Mrs. Jeffrey Harding
Sheldon Hayer
Dr. Frederic H. Herman
Chris and Erin Hindmarch
Dan Johnson and Randee Laskewitz
Dr. Matthias G. Kelm
Russ Marsden
Ralph Martins
Roy and Sarah McCollum
Kevin Menard
Dr. James W. Mulholland, in Memory of Mary R. Mulholland, R.N.
Plus Minus, Inc.
Patrick Rosenwald, in Honour of Greta Rosenwald
Carlos M. Rossi
Dr. Murray and Florence M. Sabrin
Richard L. Stees, Jr.
Loyd J. Stegent, President, Stegent Equity Advisors, Inc.
Emanuel Mark Strategos
Zachary L. Tatum
Dr. James H. Vernier
Richard D. and Susan Williams

The Global Currency Plot

How the Deep State Will Betray Your Freedom, and How to Prevent It

Thorsten Polleit

MISESINSTITUTE

AUBURN, ALABAMA

THE MISES INSTITUTE, founded in 1982, is an education and research center for the study of Austrian economics. In support of the school of thought represented by Ludwig von Mises, Murray N. Rothbard, Henry Hazlitt, and F.A. Hayek, we publish books and journals, sponsor student and professional conferences, and provide online education. Mises.org is a vast resource of free material for anyone in the world interested in these ideas. We advocate a radical shift in the intellectual climate, away from statism and toward a private property order.

For more information, see mises.org, write us at info@mises.org, or phone us at 1.800.OF.MISES.

The Global Currency Plot: How the Deep State Will Betray Your Freedom, and How to Prevent It was originally published in German as *Mit Geld zur Weltherrschaft. Warum unser Geld uns in einen dystopischen Weltstaat führt–und wie wir mit besserem Geld eine bessere Welt schaffen können* by Finanzbuch Verlag, München, 2020.

Published 2022 by the Mises Institute

The Mises Institute
518 West Magnolia Avenue
Auburn, Alabama 36832
mises.org

ISBN: 978-1-61016-756-7

For my father
Dr. Horst E. Polleit
1934–2018

PRAISE FOR THIS BOOK

Socialism is based on bureaucratic planning. This means a restriction of personal freedom. The dream of equality, a goal even of democratically dressed up socialism, can only be achieved by coercion. With clear logic Thorsten Polleit shows in this important work the aims and ways in which democratic socialism moves toward a globally planned state, dominated by a 'nomenclatura'. With convincing logic, however, he also presents the free market economy as a superior alternative. A fascinating book!

— **H.S.H. PRINCE MICHAEL VON UND ZU LIECHTENSTEIN**

"A really great achievement."

— **DR. HANS-HERMANN HOPPE, THE PROPERTY AND FREEDOM SOCIETY**

Is there a connection between political centralization, mass immigration and the quest for a common currency? Yes. Thorsten Polleit exposes with captivating logic the destructive power of democratic socialism, its tools and its aspirations for world domination. Both an enlightening and cautionary book. Essential reading!

— **MALTE FISCHER, CHIEF ECONOMIST OF WIRTSCHAFTSWOCHE**

A minimum of theoretically sound knowledge that enables us to grasp the content, the significance and the impact of the dominant socio-economic systems of our times is the precondition of any meaningful discussion. All readers, whatever their political views, will find much to stimulate their thinking in Thorsten Polleit's new book. His breadth and scope, the stark nature of his arguments and his eye for absurdity will provoke both thought and emotions. Polleit, once again helps us think more clearly about today's pressing issues.

— **KURT R. LEUBE, ACADEMIC DIRECTOR OF THE EUROPEAN CENTER OF AUSTRIAN ECONOMICS**

If you want to understand what is really happening in politics and in the international monetary system, you have to read this book!

— **ANDREAS MARQUART, CHAIRMAN OF THE LUDWIG VON MISES INSTITUTE GERMANY**

A global economy requires a global currency.

– **PAUL VOLCKER**

People are annoyed that the truth is so simple.

– **JOHANN WOLFGANG VON GOETHE**

It is never too late to become reasonable and wise; but if the insight comes late, there is always more difficulty in starting the change.

– **IMMANUEL KANT**

CONTENTS

INTRODUCTION

Every action is right which in itself, or in the maxim on which it proceeds, is such that it can coexist along with the freedom of the will of each and all in action, according to a universal law.[1]

– **IMMANUEL KANT**

On June 18, 2019, Facebook, the US social media giant, announced that it intended to issue a *global currency* in mid-2020. It was to be called *Libra*. Large US companies were said to be behind the project, such as Mastercard, Visa, PayPal, Stripe, eBay, Coinbase, Andreessen Horowitz, and Uber. Is a global *money revolution* in the offing? Will there soon be a global currency offered by private companies? On August 23, 2019, the governor of the Bank of England, Mark Carney, declared that financial markets and economies must reduce their dependence on the US dollar. He suggested that the central banks issue a common digital world currency (the "synthetic hegemonic currency").

These ventures pave the way for this book. For they indicate how relevant the thoughts presented in it are to current affairs. They are based on a central insight: if there were a global system of free markets in which everyone could freely buy what they wanted to buy, and in which producers could freely produce what consumers wanted, then there would also be a *free market for money*, and—through a voluntary agreement of all parties—a single *world currency* would emerge.

This is because that would be economically optimal. If everyone in the world uses the same money, the productive effect of money is exploited to the full: the *economic calculation* carried out with money—calculating with money prices—is thus *optimized* for everyone. By having a voluntarily

[1] Immanuel Kant, *The Science of Right*, trans. W. Hastie (1790; Marxists.org, 2003), https://www.marxists.org/reference/subject/ethics/kant/morals/ch04.htm.

chosen world currency the global division of labor, the productivity of production, and world trade would be supported in the best possible way and, as a result, people nationally and internationally would cooperate peacefully and productively.

Our current worldwide system, however, is *not one* of free markets, but rather an inhibited, restricted economic and social system. Everything is decisively co-determined and co-controlled by governments, be it upbringing, education, transport, health, law, security, old-age provision, environmental protection, or, above all, money and credit. Nothing happens without the governments' consent, requirements, and orders—whether in the United States, Japan, Europe, or Latin America. This is no coincidence: *democratic socialism* unites them all. In recent decades this *ideology* has risen to become the world's most powerful in political terms.

Democratic socialism encourages all those who follow it to gradually abolish the system of free markets and replace it with a state-run economy of control and command, a planned economy. Many special interests have gathered behind democratic socialism, some of which seem to pursue very different goals: proponents of the welfare state, social market economists, interventionists, anticapitalists, Christian socialists, state socialists, syndicalists, cultural Marxists, environmental activists, ecologists, political globalists, Keynesians, and whatever else they're all called. What unites them is the willingness or explicit goal to smash the system of free markets—or what is left of them—to pieces.

The program of democratic socialism is not limited to the national or regional level. By its very nature it claims *worldwide validity*, aims at *world domination*, a *world government*, a *world state*, and, in the language of the philosopher Karl Jaspers (1883–1969), the "peace of a despotism."[2] The world state that is the subject of this book is essentially what Jaspers calls the *world empire*:

> It is world peace through a single force that conquers all from one place on earth. It holds itself up by force. It forms the leveled masses through total planning and terror. A unified worldview is forced upon everyone in simple outlines by propaganda. Censorship and control of mental activities forces them into the respective plan, which can be modified at any time.[3]

[2] Karl Jaspers, *Vom Ursprung und Ziel der Geschichte* (Munich: Piper, 1988), p. 246.

The insight that emerges from the explanations in the following chapters is that the advocates of democratic socialism are working—some consciously, many presumably unconsciously—toward the creation of a *world government*, a *world state*. But this can only be achieved if a single *world currency*, controlled by the states, is launched beforehand. The prospect that this project could succeed must worry anyone who desires freedom and prosperity for himself and his fellow human beings. A world state, built on the principles of democratic socialism, is a *dystopia*; it would mean political tyranny and economic impoverishment, probably even starvation for countless people in the world.

This is basically nothing more than the attempt to create a *unified civilization;* the biblical image of the Tower of Babel immediately comes to mind (Gen. 11: 1–9). People have tried before to create *one* world through the power of their own ability. By constructing a tower which was to reach into heaven, they wanted to take hold of the control points of power and advance to the divine. But God prevented this because he saw that, due to their hubris, people were on the verge of losing their essence and their own selves. He recognized that their moral ability did not keep pace with their technical ability, that moral power had not grown with the ability of people to make and destroy. God intervened against this kind of union and created a different world: not one of uniformity, but a world of diversity in which people in their individuality can join together to create unity.

The thoughts which lead to this assessment and which are explained in this book claim to be strictly *logical* or *a priori*. What is meant by the term *a priori* theory? The term a priori means that something is evident, that it can be regarded as true and universal, independent of experience, such as the statement "If *a* is greater than *b*, and *b* is greater than *c*, then *a* is also greater than *c*." The term *theory* refers to a *system* of scientifically based statements that depicts excerpts from reality and explains and conclusively connects the underlying laws.

The a priori theory helps uncover the expansion dynamics of democratic socialism, which for decades has worked its way up to becoming the world's dominant ideology: it can clarify how democratic socialism shapes the state; why the state claims the monopoly of money and how it obtains it; how the state influences economic and social life with sovereignty over money; and what will happen if the path taken for decades

[3] Ibid.

continues unswervingly. From this point of view, the thoughts expressed in this book claim to provide a reliable *conditional* sketch of the future.

The a priori theory can also serve to outline the possible alternative to democratic socialism: the *private law society*. This is the logical solution and the way to put an end to the destructive work of democratic socialism.

Democratic socialism's claim to world domination does not mean that it is necessarily put into practice or can be realized. There is no compelling reason to be pessimistic. At the same time, people's thinking and actions must essentially change so that democratic socialism does not ultimately win the day and achieve world domination.

Ultimately, it is *ideas* (or *theories*) that guide people's actions. Ideas determine what is considered good and evil, just and unjust, feasible and impossible. However, human action will only be successful if the ideas that guide it are compatible with the *laws* that undoubtedly exist in the field of human action. It is therefore crucial to change the ideas prevailing today, if the *dystopia* of a political world currency and a world state is to be prevented. This requires putting the dominant ideas to the test in a rigorous intellectual discourse and, if they do not withstand critical examination, debunking them and rejecting them as false.

"There is no global anthem, no global currency, no certificate of global citizenship." These words were spoken in Ohio on December 1, 2016, by US president Donald J. Trump (b. 1946), who had promised his voters to "Make America Great Again." He was effectively elected to break the "elite," "the establishment," to deconstruct the administrative state ("deep state"), to reject "political globalism," and to embrace nationalism. At the United Nations gathering on September 24, 2019, he noted: "The free world must embrace its national foundations. It must not attempt to erase them or replace them." In the coronavirus crisis, however, even the Trump administration opted to fight the consequences of the politically dictated "lockdown" with a gigantic bailout package—out of fear that otherwise the financial and economic system would have collapsed, fully aware that this policy effectively empowers rather than deconstructs the "deep state" and the establishment. This episode is indicative of how tremendously difficult it has already become to escape from the economic and political trajectory that the ideology of democratic socialism has put into place.

In this book, the *logic of human action* serves as an impartial judge to grasp and assess the consequences, the dynamics of the development of democratic socialism, taking into account the concrete circumstances that democratic socialism happens upon and itself brings about.

This book is primarily intended for non-economists and any other interested parties. But perhaps it will also appeal to experts with strong opinions who want to open themselves to the arguments expanded upon here and then carry them further. In any case, I hope that reading this book will be of benefit to all who are interested—that it will be illuminating and inspire them to critically challenge and rethink preconceived ideas.

I would like to take this opportunity to thank many people without whose influence, criticism, advice, encouragement, and challenges this book would probably not have been possible. There are too many names for me to list and honor properly. However, I would like to take this opportunity to thank Dr. Ruth Polleit-Riechert for her support, understanding, and unwavering love.

THORSTEN POLLEIT
KÖNIGSTEIN IM TAUNUS,
OCTOBER 2019

SUMMARY

INTRODUCTION

Democratic socialism—the ideology that dominates the world today—aspires to become a world state. The route toward it requires a single world currency to be created. That would undoubtedly create a dystopia. Might this become a reality? And if so, how can it be averted? This book aims to find answers to these questions.

PART 1

1. Concerning Right Thinking: Logic

The arguments in this book claim to be strictly logical. For a better understanding, a few basics of logic—the doctrine of correct thinking—are presented. These show the possibility of making use of the incorruptible power of judgment.

2. What We Know for a Fact: Humans Act

The phrase "humans act" is logically undeniably true; it applies a priori. From it further true statements can be derived—so-called action categories—which help to think through the political-economic questions raised in this book with impartiality.

3. What is Indispensable for Human Action: Private Property

Private property is not an arbitrary variable, as many believe. It is a category of human action and cannot be denied without contradiction; unconditional respect for property also proves to be an ethically convincing norm of action.

4. Interpreting History: The Role of Theory

To understand history, one must necessarily resort to theories; without theory, there is no grasp of reality. The insights provided by a priori theory are an indispensable ingredient in the unbiased interpretation of historical events.

5. Driving Force of Civilization: Inequality

The prerequisite for peaceful and productive cooperation, and economic and cultural human progression, is humans' inequality with regard to their abilities and goals. This is also a logical insight regarding action, and it explains the process of civilizing humanity.

6. The Perfection of Exchange: Money

The modern economy and society based on the division of labor are particularly fostered when people use money. Money developed spontaneously in the free market without the intervention of a state, and having a currency for the whole world would be economically optimal.

7. The Decivilizing Force: The State

The state is a territorial monopolist with ultimate decision-making power over all conflicts in its territory. It doesn't solve interpersonal conflicts; rather, it is the cause of many and increasing numbers of social disputes.

8. The State and the Deterioration of Money: From Commodity to Fiat Money

Out of self-interest, the state obtains the monopoly over the production of money, and by force it replaces commodity money with its own fiat money. As a result, its power expands enormously, thereby becoming basically uncontrollably large.

9. Anatomy of Disruption: What Fiat Money Causes

State fiat money suffers from economic and ethical defects: it hampers economic progress and is socially unjust. Fiat money leads to a "transvaluation of all values." It is not compatible with a liberal and prosperous economy and society.

10. A Destructive Ideology: Democratic Socialism

Democratic socialism has become the dominant ideology worldwide. It relativizes and undermines property in many ways, making the state increasingly powerful, thus destroying the conditions for free and prosperous social and economic life.

11. Impact Assessment: A Case for the A Priori Theory

The a priori theory can be used to reliably estimate the consequences of human actions: it can be used to derive conditional statements about the future that are valid under specific conditions, and it can also be used to trace action–logical path dependencies.

PART 2

12. The Progression Theorem: Toward a World Government

States want to expand their power internally and externally. This applies above all to states that follow democratic socialism: they are working toward creating a worldwide uniform democratic socialism, a uniform world state with a uniform fiat world currency.

13. The Nation: Community of Language and Values

The nations–the language and value communities–are an impediment to democratic socialism's aspiration of establishing a unified world state. Therefore, democratic socialists try to vanquish the nations, and especially the principle of nationality.

14. Migration: Natural and Unnatural

The proponents of democratic socialism use migration as a means to abolish nations and the nation-state and to pave the way for a worldwide democratic socialism under a unified leadership. But this will not be achieved by a politicized migration.

15. The Illusion of Democracy: The "Iron Law of Oligarchy"

As in every democracy, an oligarchic elite rule is also formed in democratic socialism. It has a particularly strong incentive to create a uniform fiat world currency in order to come closer to the goal of creating a uniform world government, a world state.

16. US Dollar Imperialism: The Bretton Woods system

The Bretton Woods system was the first attempt to establish a single politicized world currency. It was doomed to fail because the nations had sufficient room for maneuver to escape the abuse made possible by the Bretton Woods system.

17. The Campaign against Currency Choice: The Euro

In Europe, states have succeeded in abolishing the last remnants of monetary competition and introducing a single currency. This example shows how a political world currency can be created: with the irrevocable fixing of exchange rates between national currencies.

18. The Secret and Sinister Power: The World Central Bank Cartel

The national central banks form an international cartel in line with the democratic socialists' ideas. Their monetary policy is making the global financial and economic system increasingly dependent on a globally unified monetary policy, the logical end of which is a unified world currency.

19. Blueprints for a Single World Currency: Bancor, Unitas, US Dollar, INTOR, and the Libra

There are many specific proposals to create a single world currency—brought about by a political decision, not by free market forces, for the democratic socialists want a monopolized single fiat world currency.

20. The Dystopia: A Single Fiat World Currency

A single fiat world currency would threaten freedom and prosperity on this planet to an extent that many probably cannot even imagine: with a single fiat world currency, the path would be open to a totalitarian world state.

21. Technological Disruption: Cryptocurrencies

The emergence of cryptocurrencies could prove to be the crucial disruption and achieve what economic and ethical insight has not yet been able to achieve: the opening of a free market for money, and making it impossible to establish a world state.

22. A Ray of Hope: Free Market for Money and Private Law Society

A free market for money provides people with the best possible money. It would also effectively put an end to the freedom-destroying program of democratic socialism and make possible a private law society, in which the same law applies to all.

EPILOGUE: A Better World Is Possible

We have been walking the ominous path toward a world state with a fiat world currency for decades. It is not an inevitable result, but to prevent it, essential things have to change. These will include rejecting false doctrines in modern social and economic theory and firmly reestablishing the a priori theory.

PART ONE

CHAPTER 1

CONCERNING RIGHT THINKING: LOGIC

Logic is the anatomy of thought.
– **JOHN LOCKE**

Logic is the doctrine of right thinking. It does not tell us *what* to think, but *how* to think in order to achieve the right results, arrive at the right conclusions. Logic as a science, traces its roots to the Greek philosopher Aristotle (384–322 BC); he called it "analytics." According to Aristotle, the most important elements of correct thinking are *concepts*, *judgments*, *conclusion*, and *proof*.[4] The *concepts* are the basic elements of thinking. They are obtained through definitions: the object to be defined is assigned to a class of objects whose characteristics *correspond* to those of the object to be defined. Example: A human is a living being. In addition, the definition must indicate how the object–the human–*differs* from the other objects of the class–the living beings. So, a human is a *rational* living being. Definitions (in the case of "a human") must therefore have a common (the living being) and a separating (rational) characteristic (or several).

Concepts are linked to form *judgments* (or: *statements* or *sentences*). Each judgment combines at least two concepts: *subject* and *predicate*. The subject is the concept about which something is said, the predicate denotes what is said about the concept. Example: "Gold is yellow." "Gold" is the subject, "yellow" the predicate. Individual judgments are combined to form conclusions and derive a new judgment from other judgments. A conclusion consists of the preconditions (premises) and the conclusion derived from these.

Aristotle's syllogism is central. It consists of three elements: there is a (general) major premise ("All men are mortal") and a (special) minor

[4] See Hans Joachim Störig, *Kleine Weltgeschichte der Philosophie* (Frankfurt am Main: S. Fischer Verlag GmbH, 2004), pp. 197ff.

premise ("Aristotle is a man"). The conclusion is drawn from these two premises ("Aristotle is mortal"). Conclusions are linked to form *evidence.* A proof is the logically compelling derivation of a judgment from other judgments by conclusions. However, the judgment that proves another judgment must itself be secured.

If we think through such a chain of evidence, we reach a limit, we come to *judgments of the most general character*, which in turn can no longer be proven.[5] According to Aristotle, the rational human being has the capacity to grasp such general sentences without error. The supreme proposition is the *proposition of contradiction*: "Something that is cannot simultaneously and in the same regard not be." Later, three further principles were formulated in philosophy: the *proposition of identity* ("*a* equals *a*"), the *proposition of the excluded third* ("Between being and non-being of the same object there is no third option") and the *proposition of the sufficient reason* ("No fact may be considered correct without there being a sufficient reason for it").

Since Aristotle, logic has been a central element in gaining and judging *knowledge*: knowledge gained through experience or insight. If we want to derive knowledge from experience—from observation—this is called *induction.* However, this raises the *induction problem.* Example: in the eighteenth century people knew only of the existence of white swans. It was concluded that there were only white swans. But then black swans were discovered in Australia—and the previous assumption turned out to be wrong.

This means no generalizations, no universally valid statements can be derived from individual experiences.[6] We cannot accept such an *induction conclusion* per se as valid and justify it logically. If it were valid per se, then—as far as we assume correct observations—there should never be wrong conclusions. But this is exactly what happens again and again! Moreover, the induction conclusion cannot be justified on the basis of experience. For then one would have to claim that the induction conclusion is valid because so far there have been no observable results that contradicted it. But then we would assume that the induction conclusion is already true, circumvent the problem of justification, and end up with infinite regression.

[5] E.g., W. Stanley Jevons writes, in *Elementary Lessons in Logic: Deductive and Inductive* (London, 1888), p. 3: "The laws of thought are natural laws with which we have no power to interfere."

[6] See Hans Poser, *Wissenschaftstheorie: Eine philosophische Einführung* (Stuttgart: Philipp Reclam jun., 2001), pp. 108–19.

It should also be noted that a strict distinction must be made between *truth* and *probability*. It is often assumed that we approach the truth if there is just a high probability that a particular event will occur. Here we equate the probability $w = 1$ with truth, the probability $w = 0$ with falsehood. But (logically) this notion is wrong.

Let us revisit the example of the white swans. Although so far only white swans had been observed (the probability that white swans could be observed was therefore $w = 1$), it only took one observation of a black swan to unmask as false the inductive conclusion that there were only white swans (so that actually $w = 0$). We may *not* deduce truth from a high probability.

Deduction means that we want to gain knowledge by inferring the *special* from the *general*: we derive a statement (conclusion) from other propositions (premises), as the following example illustrates:

All swans are white.
This animal is a swan.
This animal is white.

"All swans are white" and "this animal is a swan" are the premises, and "this animal is white" is the conclusion. In geometry, for example, theorems (conclusions) are derived from premises. The deductive method guarantees that the conclusions are *true* if the premises are *true*. But how do we arrive at true premises? How can premises be recognized as right or wrong?

If it is possible to find a *true* premise, which furthermore also corresponds to the reality of life, then it is possible in the course of logical deduction to derive from it further true statements about the real world. In this context, the Austrian economist Ludwig von Mises (1881–1973) achieved a successful epistemological breakthrough in the social and economic sciences—which, however, has received far too little attention and appreciation to this day.

Mises convincingly argued that *economics is not an empirical science*, but that it can only be understood (*conceptualized*) and practiced without contradiction as an *a priori science of action*. The starting point underlying Mises's deliberations—the Archimedean point, so to speak—is the seemingly trivial-sounding sentence "Humans act." But this sentence has a great significance: it is undeniably (apodictically) true. One cannot negate the sentence "Humans act" without already assuming its validity. The findings that can be derived from this are explained in more detail in the following chapter.

CHAPTER 2

WHAT WE KNOW FOR A FACT: HUMANS ACT

Like logic and mathematics,
praxeological knowledge is in us;
it does not come from without.
– **LUDWIG VON MISES**

Generally speaking, human action means replacing a state which the actor considers less advantageous with a state which is considered more advantageous. The phrase "Humans act" may sound trivial, but it by no means is. It cannot be denied without contradiction. Anyone who says, "Humans do *not* act," acts—and thus contradicts his statement. We cannot logically say or think without contradiction that humans do not act. The sentence "Humans act" therefore applies *a priori*.[7]

The expression *a priori* stands for experience-independent knowledge, for knowledge that, with strict necessity, is valid: something is as it is and not different; it allows no exception and can therefore claim unrestricted validity. Plato and Aristotle were among the first to distinguish real knowledge (*episteme*) from mere opinion (*doxa*).[8] In this sense, the doctrine of human action can be described as an *a priori science of action*: the sentence "Humans act" is undeniably true, and further true knowledge can be derived from it by deduction.[9]

---

[7] A priori statements can be realized in advance, that is, before any perception, as true or false. They are not concerned with the temporal dimension between perception and statement, but with the role of perception in justifying statements. An a priori statement can be substantiated or rejected (refuted) independently of perceptions.

[8] See Otfried Höffe, *Immanuel Kant: Eine philosophische Einführung* (Stuttgart: Philipp Reclam jun., 2001), pp. 57–63, esp. 58.

[9] On the logic of action, see Ludwig von Mises, *Nationalökonomie: Theorie des Handelns und Wirtschaftens* (Geneva: Edition Union, 1940), pp. 11–114; Murray N. Rothbard, *Man, Economy, and State, with Power and Market*, 2d scholar's ed. (Auburn, AL: Ludwig von Mises Institute, 2009) chap. 1; "Praxeology as the Method of the Social Sciences" in *Economic Controversies* (Auburn, AL: Ludwig von Mises Institute, 2011), pp. 29–58; and "Praxeology: The Methodology of Austrian

The sentence "Humans act" is not open to any *ultimate justification.* We cannot prove it by resorting to further justifications. In that sense it's an ultimate *given.* The phrase "Humans act" is a precondition which must always be made use of and which cannot be denied when we act (for example, it is made use of when we dispute something). For this reason, the realization that humans act can serve as a true, logically undisputable starting point of scientific thought.

Human action is determined by *ideas*—in the sense of thoughts or theories.[10] This, too, is an insight that can be derived without contradiction from the logic of human action. For it to be denied, it would have to be shown that human action is systematically determined by external, observable (chemical, biological, or physical) factors. But this has not yet been achieved—and it is also logically unthinkable that this will ever happen.[11]

Human action always takes place under two conditions. One is that the actor feels dissatisfaction with the present condition. If he were content, there would be no reason for him to strive for change, and he would not act—but as has already become clear, this is not imaginable without contradictions. The other condition is that the actor is of the opinion that he can alleviate the dissatisfaction, perhaps even completely eliminate it, by his actions. If it weren't for that, he wouldn't act. But since no one cannot *not* act, the opinion of the actor that he can achieve his goals through action is a necessary condition for every action.

Human action is always *individual action.* Only individuals (the word comes from Latin and means "indivisible particle") act. Groups or collectives do not act. They can always conceptually be traced back to their individual participants and their actions.

Human action is *goal oriented*: It is intended to achieve aims and purposes. This, too, cannot be denied without becoming involved in a contradiction, because saying, "Humans do not act purposefully," is ultimately also a form of purposeful action. So anyone who says that human action is not purposeful is committing a contradiction.

Economics," in *Economic Controversies*, pp. 59–80; Hans-Hermann Hoppe, "On Praxeology and the Praxeological Foundation of Epistemology," in *The Economics and Ethics of Private Property: Studies in Political Economy and Philosophy*, 2d ed. (Auburn, AL: Ludwig von Mises Institute, 2006), pp. 265–94.

[10] See Ludwig von Mises, *Theory and History: An Interpretation of Social and Economic Evolution* (Auburn, AL: Ludwig von Mises Institute, 1957), p. 3f. and 64.

[11] See also, for example, Holm Tetens, *Geist, Gehirn, Maschine: Philosophische Versuche über ihren Zusammenhang* (Stuttgart: Philipp Reclam jun., 1994).

Human action can consist in doing something visible to all, or in omitting something consciously, not always visible to outsiders. Human action can be distinguished from purely *reflexive action* (which is expressed, for example, in the form of winking or a cry of pain). For example, to the extent that the actor suppresses a reflex, he expands the scope of his goal-oriented action.

From the undeniably true sentence "Humans act" further true statements can be derived in a logical and deductive way—these are the basic terms of human experience, or *categories*. For example, the realization that humans act presupposes a cause-and-effect relationship (*causality*). The fact that action is taken implies causality: if there were no cause-and-effect relationship, a human could not act; he would have no prospect of being able to achieve his goals through action.

Action requires the use of *means* (one can also say *commodities*). Commodities are necessarily scarce: *scarcity* is a logical realization of action. If means were not scarce, human action would not be dependent on them. They wouldn't have to be rationed, and they wouldn't be means.

Every action takes *time*. It is a means that the actor must use to achieve goals. If action could be taken without a temporal extension, the goals that the actor strives for would be instantly achieved—and he could not act, which however, as we have seen, is unthinkable; that is, action that takes no time is unthinkable.

Because action always requires time, and because time is a means of achieving goals, the actor prefers to achieve his goals earlier rather than later. This means that his *time preference* is always and everywhere positive. Currently available goods are valued higher than goods (of the same type and quality and under the same conditions) that are only available later. Future goods therefore suffer a reduction in value compared with goods currently available. The *originary interest* represents this discount. Time preference and its manifestation, the *originary interest rate* (*Urzins*), are *elementary value phenomena* of human action; they cannot disappear.

In the field of human action there is no *balance* in the sense of a state of rest, an unchanging situation. For that would mean that humans no longer act—and we cannot think that without contradicting ourselves. By acting, humans can come closer to the desired state. But there can be no final attainment of a state of equilibrium, of "complete satisfaction."

Human action takes place under *uncertainty*. Experience has shown that we don't know everything about the future: for example, we don't know today which companies and which products there will be in the future. There is a logical reason why human action takes place in uncertainty: if there were no uncertainty, the actor would already know what is going to happen in the future. But then he could no longer act. His actions could no longer influence the future course of things—but it is not conceivable without contradiction that man *does not* act.[12]

It has already been stated that scarcity is a category of human action. The sentence "Humans act" therefore also includes the two following perceptions: (1) The greater the stock of goods that the actor has, the greater the (marginal) benefit that the stock of goods provides. This is because goods are scarce and a larger stock of goods allows more goals to be achieved. (2) The *marginal utility* provided by an additional unit of goods decreases with increasing stock. The first available unit of a good is used to satisfy the most pressing need. The second available unit of the good is used to satisfy the most pressing of the remaining needs—which, of course, is less pressing than the previously satisfied need. And so on. Together, (1) and (2) represent the law of *diminishing marginal utility*.

Human action logically requires the category of *property*, or private property. Property is not an arbitrarily created institution—the introduction of which brought evil into the world, as Jean-Jacques Rousseau (1712–78) claimed. It is rather an a priori. Whether we like it or not, property cannot be excluded from the logic of human action. The central role that property plays in human action, and in particular in the coexistence of people in the community, will be discussed in more detail in the next chapter.

IMMANUEL KANT'S CRITIQUE OF REASON AND HUMAN ACTION

What epistemological status does the sentence "Humans act" have? To find an answer to this question, let us go back to the reflections of the Königsberg philosopher Immanuel Kant (1724–1804). Kant noted that progress in the natural sciences and empirical science was increasingly calling into question the ideal of enlightenment that he advocated—he spoke of *reasonable autonomy*. He couldn't accept that so easily. According to him, we humans can understand ourselves

[12] This does *not* mean, by the way, that everything is uncertain. If there is uncertainty in human action, there must also be certainty; certainty is the logical correlate to uncertainty.

as reasonable autonomous persons only if we adhere to the following metaphysical assumptions. Man has free will; he has an immortal soul; God is the ultimate cause of the universe; and the world is functionally tailored to man. But does metaphysics (and the assumptions based on it) qualify as science?

Metaphysics deals with questions that cannot be answered by observations (experiments)—like the question of the existence of God or the immortality of the soul. Science has it easier in this regard. Its statements can be verified by observations. Kant refers to statements that derive knowledge from experience as *a posteriori* (in retrospect). He describes experience-independent knowledge, i.e., statements that on the basis of perceptions cannot be regarded as either false or true, as *a priori*. Seen in this light, metaphysical statements must be a priori because they cannot be supported or rejected by experience.

That, however, does not yet sufficiently determine metaphysical statements. "Bodies are extended" is a sentence that is *a priori* true because it is by definition true: what constitutes bodies is that they are extended. Kant calls statements *analytic* that are true or false solely because of the meaning of the terms they contain. Empirical scientific statements that are not analytic are described by Kant as *synthetic*: "God is the final cause of the universe" is such a statement (it does not follow from the definition of "God"). Metaphysical statements are thus characterized by a second characteristic: they're also synthetic. When Kant asks whether metaphysics is possible as science, he asks about the possibility of synthetic judgments *a priori*—an investigation which he calls *transcendental*: "I call all knowledge transcendental, which does not deal with objects, but with our type of knowledge as such of objects, if this is to be possible *a priori*."[13]

Kant focuses on the possibility of the necessary conditions for being able to make objective experiences of the reality of life. According to him, only that which satisfies the conditions under which man can make experiences can be experienced by us humans: "The conditions of the possibility of experience in general are at the same time conditions of the possibility of the objects of experience, and

[13] Immanuel Kant, *Kritik der reinen Vernunft*, ed. Ingeborg Heidemann (Stuttgart: Philipp Reclam jun., 1968), p. 25.

therefore have objective validity in a synthetic judgment *a priori*."[14] The philosopher Holm Tetens (b. 1948) interprets the statement of the above quotation as follows: "There are necessary conditions of experience that come about through the exercise of our cognitive faculty. All objects of experience must meet these conditions. Therefore, the statements that claim that the objects of experience are subject to these conditions are synthetic statements *a priori*."[15]

Man therefore does not experience the objects of his experience as they are, but rather imposes on them qualities which spring from his cognitive faculty. The sentence "Humans act" can be interpreted as a necessary condition for the possibility of experience; it is condition and precondition of experience. For this reason, the categories of human action can be used to test the truth content of economic theories: theories that contradict the categories of human action must raise serious doubts as to their accuracy.[16]

Ludwig von Mises describes the doctrine of human action as *praxeology*: "The propositions of praxeology gained through consistent and error-free thinking are not only completely certain and indisputable like the propositions of mathematics; they refer with all their certainty and indisputability to action as it is practiced in life and in reality. Praxeology therefore conveys exact knowledge of real things."[17] With praxeological thinking, with the logic of action, we can also counter the *criticism of idealism* that Kant's theory was and is exposed to; see the explanations in the appendix of this book.

[14] Ibid., p. 197.

[15] Holm Tetens, *Kants "Kritik der reinen Vernunft": Ein systematischer Kommentar* (Stuttgart: Philipp Reclam jun., 2006), pp. 35–36.

[16] The logic of action makes the attempts to identify economic theories as right or wrong *decidable issues of truth*, to adopt the philosopher Rolf W. Puster, "Dualismen und ihre Hintergründe," in *Theorie und Geschichte: Eine Interpretation sozialer und wirtschaftlicher Entwicklung*, by Ludwig von Mises (Munich: H. Akston Verlags GmbH, 2014), pp. 7–50, esp. 31.

[17] Mises, *Nationalökonomie*, p. 20.

CHAPTER 3

WHAT IS INDISPENSABLE FOR HUMAN ACTION: PROPERTY

There can be no happiness without constancy and prudence.[18]
– LUCIUS ANNAEUS SENECA

In the indisputably true sentence that cannot be denied without contradiction, "Humans act," something is assumed, something is presupposed, which deserves very special attention, but is all too often overlooked or even called into question, and that is *property*—understood as the property of everyone in his own body (*self-ownership*) and the property in external goods which one has acquired in a nonaggressive way. This statement will be explained and justified in more detail below, with reference to the *a priori argumentation* as formulated by the philosophers Karl-Otto Apel (1922–2017) and Jürgen Habermas (b. 1929).[19]

Arguing means asserting something with the intention of convincing the interlocutor of the correctness or falsity of a fact.[20] Examples of this are "I am right about this" or "Everything is uncertain, and that is certain." Arguing is a particular, special form of human action. The special thing about the sentence "Humans argue" is that it cannot be disputed without contradiction. It applies *a priori*; it is evident: whoever says, "Humans do not argue," argues and thus contradicts what has been said.

[18] Francis and Henry Hazlitt, *The Wisdom of the Stoics* (Lanham, MD: University Press of America, 1984), p. 15.

[19] See Karl-Otto Apel, "Das Apriori der Kommunikationsgemeinschaft und die Grundlagen der Ethik," in *Transformation der Philosophie*, 2 vols. (Frankfurt am Main: Suhrkamp, 1973); and Jürgen Habermas, *Moralbewußtsein und kommunikatives Handeln* (Frankfurt am Main: Suhrkamp, 1983).

[20] On this issue, see Hans-Hermann Hoppe, "On the Ultimate Justification of the Ethics of Private Property," in *The Economics and Ethics of Private Property* (Auburn, AL: Ludwig von Mises Institute, 2006), pp. 339–45, esp. 339ff. and "The Justice of Economic Efficiency," in *The Economics and Ethics of Private Property*, pp. 331–38, esp. 331ff.

Arguing, like every form of human action, requires the use of scarce resources. In the simplest case, anyone who argues has to use his body: to open his mouth and make his vocal cords vibrate. So anyone who argues needs at least ownership of his own body, *self-ownership*. Without controlling his own body, the actor cannot argue. Human action necessarily presupposes physicality.

But those who argue do not only presuppose self-ownership for themselves. They also assume it for the person with whom they argue. Anyone who argues assumes that his counterpart either shares his arguments, approves them in part, or perhaps even rejects them. The person with whom one argues must also have self-ownership, for otherwise he cannot argue—and we have already recognized that one cannot *not* argue.

If we cannot deny that the actor has self-ownership of his own body without falling into contradiction, then the necessity for the actor to preserve his body (as created by nature) follows directly from this. To this end, the actor must be able to acquire *external goods* such as food, clothing, and housing. Property—self-ownership and ownership of external goods needed to preserve one's body—can thus be regarded without contradiction as an *a priori category* of human action.

At this point, another question arises: How is ownership—ownership of one's own body and ownership of external goods—to be judged *from an ethical point of view*? Ethics—also known as moral philosophy—deals with the question: What is a *right* action and how can it be *justified*? It may come as a surprise, but economics has more to contribute to ethics than one might initially assume. Ethics finds its starting point in an irrevocable economic realization: that human life takes place under *scarcity*.

If there were no scarcity of resources to be deployed to help those actors achieve their goals, ethical questions—such as what is right, what is wrong—would not arise in the first place. In such a world there would be no interpersonal conflicts. For example, if there were no scarcity and Mr. *A* consumed a banana, he would not diminish his present or future banana supply. Nor would his consuming the banana limit the current and future consumption of bananas by Mr. *B* and Mrs. *C*. But human action always takes place—and this is necessarily assumed—under scarcity.

In a world of scarcity, how can the actor procure the necessary goods so that there is no conflict with the property of others? This is only possible in three nonaggressive ways: (1) domestication of natural resources that have not previously been claimed by anyone else ("homesteading"); (2) production, i.e., "mixing" one's own labor with natural resources; and (3) voluntary exchange, including gifting. Anyone who appropriates goods in one of these three ways acquires property without violating the property of his fellow human beings.

Is human action characterized by unconditional respect for property ethically acceptable? In order to answer this question, we must first consider the requirements to be met by an *ethical rule of action*.[21] Firstly, an ethical rule of action must apply equally to everyone at all times and everywhere. This requirement is expressed, for instance, in Kant's *categorical imperative*: "Act only according to that maxim whereby you can at the same time will that it should become a universal law."[22] In addition to this requirement of universality ("universalizability"), an ethical rule must, secondly, ensure that its observance preserves human existence in principle. If this were not ensured, sooner or later there would be no need for ethics. An example: the rule "Everyone drinks five bottles of schnapps a day" can in principle be made the default for everyone. But it would certainly not ensure the survival of those who follow this rule, but rather endanger it. But what, precisely, can and must an ethical rule look like?

The US economist and social philosopher Murray N. Rothbard (1926–95) dealt with this question. With reference to the natural law argumentation of John Locke (1632–1704), Rothbard develops the following train of thought. We assume that there is Mr. *A* and Mr. *B*. In the *first case*, Mr. *A* owns Mr. *B*. So, Mr. *A* is the master and Mr. *B* is his slave. This rule cannot be ethical. Mr. *A* and Mr. *B* may well survive under this rule. But the rule cannot be ethical, because obviously there is a different rule for Mr. *A* than for Mr. *B*.

In the *second case*, Mr. *A* and Mr. *B* own each other: Mr. *A* owns Mr. *B*, and at the same time Mr. *B* owns Mr. *A*. That cannot be an ethical rule either. It does indeed apply to both equally. But this rule cannot guarantee the survival of Messrs. *A* and *B*. In order to be able to do anything, Mr. *A* must have Mr. *B*'s consent. But Mr. *A* cannot get it, because Mr. *B*, so that he can himself act, must first obtain and receive Mr. *A*'s approval. The rule

[21] See Murray N. Rothbard, *The Ethics of Liberty* (New York: New York University Press, 1998), pp. 45–50; see also the introduction by Hoppe, esp. pp. xvi–xvii.

[22] Immanuel Kant, *Kritik der praktischen Vernunft* (Stuttgart: Philipp Reclam jun., 1961), pp. 50, 54–55. Translation in Kant, *Grounding for the Metaphysics of Morals*, trans. James W. Ellington (Indianapolis, IN: Hackett Publishing Company, 1993), p. 30.

that each belongs to the other, that all belong to each other, leads to the downfall of all.

In the *third case*, Mr. *A* and Mr. *B* each own themselves. This rule proves to be ethically acceptable. It can be used for anyone and everyone, anytime and anywhere. It also ensures in principle the consideration of those who adhere to it. Human action, which is characterized by absolute respect for property—understood as self-ownership and property acquired in a nonaggressive way—thus fulfills the requirements of ethical action.

Rothbard derives his *rational ethics* from a consideration of natural law. Not surprisingly, this "line of argument" has not been without its criticism. Hans-Hermann Hoppe (b. 1949) subsequently provided Rothbard's position, that unconditional respect for property qualifies as an ethical rule of action, with an a priori justification. It was Hoppe who—as explained at the beginning of this chapter—conceptualized property as an *a priori category* of human action by means of *a priori reasoning*. What epistemological consequences this has will occupy us in the coming chapters. Prior to that, however, we want to gain clarity about the logic of human action in the sense of a *metatheory*. This is done in the following chapter.

CHAPTER 4

INTERPRETING HISTORY: THE ROLE OF THEORY

But though all our knowledge begins with experience, it does not follow that it all arises from experience.[23]

— IMMANUEL KANT

There is no comprehension of real events, of the reality of life, without theory. In order to recognize something like "interest," "money supply" or "gross national product," for example, one has to base one's analysis on a theory; a theory that combines the "diversity of phenomena" in a systematic and consistent way. The fact that theory is indispensable for our knowledge of world events, however, is repeatedly overlooked and even questioned with fervor. Immanuel Kant pointed out this mistake in his essay "On the Old Saw: That May Be Right in Theory but It Won't Work in Practice" as early as 1793.

Man must necessarily resort to theories in order to recognize reality. He cannot think without theory. Ludwig von Mises made this clear: "Thinking and acting are inseparable. Every action is always based on a definite idea about causal relations. He who thinks a causal relation thinks a theorem. Action without thinking, practice without theory are unimaginable. The reasoning may be faulty and the theory incorrect; but thinking and theorizing are not lacking in any action."[24]

Economic theories are not vain academic basic exercises, not abstract games. Rather, they have great practical relevance. This can be seen, for example, in the interpretation of experiences of historical economic or social events, which are nothing more than past human actions. History is not a finished book, not an objective book, but its material, its testimonies in speech and writing, must be laid out and interpreted. Seen

[23] Immanuel Kant, *Critique of Pure Reason*, trans. Marcus Weigelt (London: Penguin Books, 2007).

[24] Ludwig von Mises, *Human Action: A Treatise on Economics*, scholar's ed. (Auburn, AL: Ludwig von Mises Institute, 1998), p. 177.

in this light, historical science is an understanding *science*: its task is to document what has happened, to make understandable the reasons why people have acted in one way or another.

Why did the Emperor Wilhelm II (1859–1941) dismiss Chancellor Otto von Bismarck (1815–98) in March 1890? What are the reasons that led many governments in the early 1970s to abolish their currencies' gold backing and use unsecured paper money? Why did the global financial and economic crisis in 2008–09 occur? Why was Trump elected forty-fifth president of the United States?

Historical events of human action must necessarily be recorded and understood with the aid of theories. This is no easy task: anyone who wants to grasp and interpret the history of human action in a meaningful way must resort to a multitude of fields of knowledge: for example, natural sciences such as biology, chemistry, and medicine, but also social sciences such as economics in particular. In other words: it is necessary to apply the *method of understanding* based on the experiential and natural sciences but also the a priori sciences of logic, mathematics, and economics, and to ensure that understanding does not conflict with the knowledge provided by the natural and a priori sciences.[25]

With regard to economics, the important question arises: Which of their theories are right and which are wrong? For only by using the right theories and eliminating the wrong ones does it become possible to learn reliable lessons from the experience of human action. False theories lead to false interpretations. Economics, understood as an a priori science of action, is particularly useful in this context: it can be understood as a *metatheory*, as a theory of theories.

With the help of the method of reflecting on logic and action, it is possible to judge beyond doubt whether an economic theory is right or wrong. An economic theory must raise doubts about its correctness or can be rejected as false if it is not consistent with the a priori categories of action. Whether an economic theory is right or wrong can be decided without first having to "try out" the economic theory in practice.[26]

---

[25] See Mises, *Nationalökonomie*, p. 55.

[26] If one were to assume, for example, that action does not require time, how would a simple supply-and-demand model be judged? If action could be taken without extending time, all the objectives pursued by the actor would be achieved immediately and instantly—and there would be no reason or possibility of acting. There would be no more action. But this cannot be thought without contradiction: humans cannot not act. For any supply-and-demand model, however simple, to be meaningful and realistic, it must explicitly or implicitly assume that any action takes place in time. Without acting in time there would be no supply-and-demand curve!

For example, by resorting to the logic of action, we can consider the following four (economic theory) statements to be true: (1) Any voluntary exchange is beneficial to all parties involved. If it were otherwise, it would not take place—human action means, after all, replacing one condition with another, more advantageous, condition. (2) The marginal utility of a good decreases with increasing stocks of goods; this also follows logically from the indisputable knowledge that humans act. (3) Minimum wages above market-clearing levels lead to involuntary unemployment. This is a direct result of the (logical) law of supply and demand. (4) If the money supply increases and the demand for money remains unchanged, the prices of goods rise and the purchasing power of money decreases; this also follows from the law of decreasing marginal utility, which can be justified logically.

One example of how a priori action science can shed light on history is the German hyperinflation which occurred in 1923, which, as is well known, almost completely destroyed the purchasing power of the German paper mark and led to a currency reform in November of the same year. For a long time, German economists cited the reparations paid to the victors of the First World War and a deficit in the German balance of payments as reasons for the massive decline in the value of Germany's money. This was mainly because at that time the social scientists and economists were blindly following the thought processes of the so-called (younger) *Historical school*, which was inseparably linked to the economist Gustav von Schmoller (1838–1917).

The Historical school took the view that there were no laws and no a priori findings in economics. For them, therefore, the economist's task was to sift through historical documents and interpret them subjectively; economists proceeded as if interpreting a literary text. No wonder that the German economists who took this academic approach blundered about more or less completely intellectually befogged and did not understand the world. The German economist Moritz J. Bonn (1873–1965) wrote about it:

> For years the economic education of the Prussian bureaucracy was in the hands of Schmoller and his students. The negative result of this became visible in the inflation crisis after the First World War. The bureaucracy had no idea of the simplest economic terms—there was hardly anyone in the Prussian or Reich Ministry of Finance who knew anything about inflation (things were different in Austria). Moreover, Schmoller's relativism had

> convinced the civil service of the insignificance of expert consultants. His students had not learned to look at the present with a view to the future, they had been taught to look backwards. They could not say what had to be done; they only knew what had been done.[27]

The economists of the Historical school were unaware that it was the out-of-control increase in the money supply by the Reichsbank that sealed the fate of the paper money market—a realization that can be drawn directly from the logic of human action! The explanation is that money is the generally accepted medium of exchange. The medium of exchange function is the core function of money, the increase in the money supply therefore leads—in accordance with the *law of diminishing marginal utility*—to a reduction in the exchange value of the monetary unit.

If the money supply increases in the hands of the market actors, then the marginal utility of the additionally received monetary unit decreases and the other goods become comparatively more valuable compared to money. The money holders then exchange their money for other goods—offer their money on the market for other goods. The consequence is that goods prices rise. And the steeper the rise of the money supply, the greater will be the effect of price increases and thus the decline in money's purchasing power. Ludwig von Mises formulated the logical a priori explanation demonstrating that the demand for money is *not independent* of the money supply or its increase as follows:

> But if once public opinion is convinced that the increase in the quantity of money will continue and never come to an end, and that consequently the prices of all commodities and services will not cease to rise, everybody becomes eager to buy as much as possible and to restrict his cash holding to a minimum size. For under these circumstances the regular costs incurred by holding cash are increased by the losses caused by the progressive fall in purchasing power. The advantages of holding cash must be paid for by sacrifices which are deemed unreasonably burdensome. This phenomenon was, in the great European inflations of the Twenties, called flight into real goods (*Flucht in die Sachwerte*) or crack-up boom (*Katastrophenhausse*).[28]

---

[27] Moritz Julius Bonn, *So macht man Geschichte* (Munich: List Verlag, 1953), pp. 53–54.
[28] Mises, *Human Action*, pp. 423–24.

The a priori science of action, however, does not only help to interpret historical individual events in a rational, scientifically objective way.[29] It also allows us to understand the social evolution, the motives for the cooperative and productive coexistence of human beings—the *process of civilization*—without having to resort to vague assumptions or metaphysical references. It also reveals that no state (as we have seen and experienced in history) was necessary for human civilization, for orderly coexistence in the community. This will be explained in more detail in the following chapter.

[29] For the principles of such an interpretation of history, see Joseph T. Salerno, Introduction to *A History of Money and Banking in the United States: The Colonial Era to World War II*, by Murray N. Rothbard (Auburn, AL: Ludwig von Mises Institute, 2002), pp. 7–43.

CHAPTER 5

THE DRIVING FORCE OF CIVILIZATION: INEQUALITY

Reason is the principle of general equality, the mind is the principle of inequality among men.
– **FRIEDRICH WILHELM JOSEPH SCHELLING**

The realization that humans act—that they cannot *not* act—makes us understand why individuals *voluntarily* cooperate with each other; why they do not constantly argue and fight with each other but seek peaceful coexistence. The logical explanation for this is that *people form a community because of the diversity of nature.* The diversity of nature means, on the one hand, that the actors are *unequal* in terms of their individual abilities, values, and goals. On the other hand, it means that they encounter different living and environmental conditions on this earth.

It is the diversity of nature—the fact that each human being is special and different from the others and that his (subjectively perceived) life circumstances are different from those of his fellow human beings—that necessarily influences the actions of each human being. It is also the diversity of nature that forces people into the *division of labor.* Anyone equipped with a minimum of reason recognizes that the division of labor promises him *higher productivity compared* to a situation in which he produces all the desired goods himself ("subsistence economy"). In addition, he comes to the conclusion that there are goals that cannot be achieved without working with other people.

For example, Mr. *A* realizes that he cannot build a bridge over the river without the help of Mr. *B* and Mr. *C*. Temporary alliances, however, are limited to a few people cooperating. A permanent division of labor, as can be observed in developed economies, *cannot* be explained by *ad hoc* cooperation. It requires a different explanation. The British economist David

Ricardo (1772–1823) developed the *theory of comparative cost advantages* to explain trade relations between countries. Ricardo shows that trade between countries is advantageous when people in each country concentrate on producing the goods that they can produce most cheaply (see chapter 13).

Ludwig von Mises saw Ricardo's theory as much more than just an explanation for international trade. He saw it as a *law of association*. By recognizing that they are better off through the division of labor compared to working in isolation, people no longer see themselves as competitors for the appropriation of scarce resources provided by nature. Rather, they come to the conclusion that their situation is improved when they divide their labor with others, not only temporarily, but permanently.

It is the difference between the actors—in terms of their abilities, wishes, and goals—that makes cooperation possible in the first place. If all those involved were the same, there would be no social cooperation. If everyone had the same abilities, wishes, and goals, nobody would be able to make use of his fellow human beings! It would mean that you too want to be where I am at the moment; you can do the same work just as well as I can; you want to tell me exactly what I want to tell you; you already know what I know. It would be dystopia!

The development of civilization can be understood with the logic of human action. Mises put it this way:

> If and as far as labor under the division of labor is more productive than isolated labor, and if and as far as man is able to realize this fact, human action itself tends toward cooperation and association; man becomes a social being not in sacrificing his own concerns for the sake of a mythical Moloch, society, but in aiming at an improvement in his own welfare. Experience teaches that this condition—higher productivity achieved under the division of labor—is present because its cause—the inborn inequality of men and the inequality in the geographical distribution of the natural factors of production—is real. Thus we are in a position to comprehend the course of social evolution.[30]

[30] Mises, *Human Action*, p. 160.

And furthermore:

> In order to comprehend why man did not remain solitary, searching like the animals for food and shelter for himself only and at most also for his consort and his helpless infants, we do not need to have recourse to a miraculous interference of the Deity or to the empty hypostasis of an innate urge toward association. Neither are we forced to assume that the isolated individuals or primitive hordes one day pledged themselves by a contract to establish social bonds. The factor that brought about primitive society and daily works toward its progressive intensification is human action that is animated by the insight into the higher productivity of labor achieved under the division of labor.[31]

The doctrine of human action, laid down by Mises, reveals another important insight: that people, despite all their differences, traditions, cultures, and beliefs, have an economic incentive to enter into peaceful and productive cooperation with one another:

> But even if such a thing as a natural and inborn hatred between various races existed, it would not render social cooperation futile and would not invalidate Ricardo's theory of association. Social cooperation has nothing to do with personal love or with a general commandment to love one another. People do not cooperate under the division of labor because they love or should love one another. They cooperate because this best serves their own interests. Neither love nor charity nor any other sympathetic sentiments but rightly understood selfishness is what originally impelled man to adjust himself to the requirements of society, to respect the rights and freedoms of his fellow men and to substitute peaceful collaboration for enmity and conflict.[32]

The logical realization that people with different abilities, desires, and goals *voluntarily* combine to form a community based on the division of labor does not mean that living together in a community does not require any rules and laws. Rather, it means that no ruler, no coercive apparatus, no central force is needed to persuade people to enter and support a community based on the division of labor. We can therefore say at this

[31] Ibid., pp. 159–60.
[32] Ibid., p. 168.

point that the free market economy—which is characterized by absolute respect for property and for the emergence and preservation of which no central coercive force is necessary—is the *natural form of human coexistence.*[33]

The logic of human action also explains the emergence of money, the *generally accepted medium of exchange*: money spontaneously emerged from the free market, from a commodity. A particularly important insight! It stands in contrast to the prevailing opinion today that the emergence of the use of money can only be explained by the fact that an authority, the state, brought about an agreement for the use of money as a means of human exchange.[34] The following chapter clears up this misconception.

---

[33] The aspect of "statelessness" will be discussed in chapter 22.

[34] This view goes back to Georg Friedrich Knapp (1842–1926) and his book *Staatliche Theorie des Geldes* (1905).

CHAPTER 6

THE PERFECTION OF EXCHANGE: MONEY

If not to make the world better, what is money for?
— **ELIZABETH TAYLOR**

The logic contained in the sentence "Humans act" explains why people seek peaceful coexistence, why they cooperate voluntarily: it is the diversity of their abilities, desires, and goals that makes them enter into a *division of labor*. Division of labor means *specialization*: everyone concentrates on the activity that they are comparatively best able to perform. As a result, people no longer produce goods exclusively for their own needs, but also, above all, goods that their fellow humans wish to ask for.

Division of labor and specialization require interpersonal exchange. The most primitive form is *barter*: everyone exchanges the goods he has produced for the goods that others have produced and which he would like to possess. However, such barter ("goods for goods") is cumbersome. After all, you always have to find someone who requires exactly what you have to offer. If this is not the case, if there is no "double coincidence" of wants, no exchange takes place.

If, however, the exchange possibilities are limited, the possibility of extending the division of labor and specialization reaches its limits: Productivity and thus prosperity are lower compared to a situation in which exchange possibilities are virtually unlimited. The possibilities for exchange can, however, be expanded if people switch to *indirect exchange*. Everyone begins to exchange his goods for those goods (indirect means of exchange) which themselves do not serve the final purpose, but which are subsequently exchanged for the ultimately desired goods.

Initially, there is a whole range of indirect means of exchange. Gradually, however, people reduce this multitude to a few means of exchange. The most widespread indirect medium of exchange becomes the generally accepted medium of exchange: *money*. Seen in this light, money is the commodity that has achieved the greatest marketability. However, money not only performs the extremely important function of a medium of exchange, it also plays another important role: money enables *economic calculation*.

In a primitive subsistence economy, in which everyone works for himself, there is no need for money. For example, a farmer working alone can judge whether he is better able to use his daily labor to clear a forest or to hunt. He can see which of these activities is most advantageous for him. In modern economies, which are organized on the basis of the division of labor and in which complex production routes have to be followed, money is indispensable, because an economic calculation cannot be carried out without money.

An economy is always faced with the question: How should the available resources (which are necessarily scarce) be used to best serve the needs? Let's take, as an example, energy supply: Should a hydro-electric power station or a coal-fired power station be built? Both projects are complex. A lot of preparatory work is needed to make hydro power usable. For example, excavators, transport capacity, and manpower must be provided before the diversion of the watercourse and the construction of a dam can begin. Considerable preparatory work is also required for the construction of a coal-fired power plant. For example, drills, pit fans, and winding towers must be provided before coal mining can begin.

Such complex decisions can be managed by using money. The monetary prices formed in the market for the individual means of production reflect the value which the market players assign to them. If, for example, the price of a good rises, this shows that it has become scarce and must be used carefully. If, for example, it turns out that the costs incurred for rectifying the watercourse cannot be covered by the expected energy prices, this means that this form of energy supply does not make economic sense, because obviously there are other, more worthwhile uses for the scarce resources. Only economic calculation, which calculates with money prices, allows the most urgent needs to be met with scarce resources and the less urgent needs to be postponed. Advanced production based on the division of labor would not be possible without money.

This insight is not limited to a single isolated economy, it can also be applied to the *world economic system.* Up to now, people have been accustomed to using national money: purchases and sales are made in US dollars in the US, in euros in the eurozone, in Chinese renminbi in China, and in Japanese yen in Japan. But economic reason tells us that these *regional monies are suboptimal* if the goal is to advance the possibility of developing the division of labor worldwide.

A world economy in which different types of money are used is still a form of *barter economy.* Economic calculation which has to cope with many currencies does not fully exploit the potential that can be achieved by using a single currency. For economic calculation, the productive power of money is optimized only when everyone uses the same money, when a uniform type of money is used throughout the world. By the way, this was already the case in the last quarter of the nineteenth century: a uniform currency was used internationally–*gold money.* It had risen to a position of being *world money*, so to speak.

Using the logic of human action, we can justify why having *one* type of money is optimal for the economy or rather for the global economy.[35] Let us assume that there is money *A* and money *B*. If both are equally good money from the point of view of the money users, one of them is expendable. If, on the other hand, money *A* is better than money *B*, money *A* is used, and money *B* is not required and is pushed out of the market. Could it be that money *A* and *B* are used side by side, if we assume we act from a position of uncertainty, meaning that the market players, because they are not quite sure whether money *A* or *B* is better, ask for both money *A* and money *B*? The answer is no.

Even in an uncertain situation, using one type of money is optimal from the point of view of economic calculation. There may be uncertainty as to whether the money used will retain its purchasing power over time; or whether it will be recovered if it is held by banks (i.e., a default or counterparty risk). However, in free markets such uncertainties are resolved contractually if necessary. For example, money users can take out inflation

[35] This thought is usually not pursued by mainstream economists. Rather, there are *ad hoc* arguments. For example, Kenneth Rogoff argues for at least three or four currencies that should be globally sustainable. (Rogoff, "Why Not a Global Currency?," *American Economic Review* 91, no. 2 (2001): 234–47.) Barry Eichengreen says a multiple currency system will emerge based on US dollars, euros, and renminbi. (Eichengreen, "Managing a Multiple Reserve Currency World" [paper prepared for the Asian Development Bank Institute/Earth Institute project Reform of the Global Monetary System, April 2010].)

and payment default insurance if they wish. Therefore, even after taking uncertainty into account, the optimal number of money types remains one. A free market for money thus amounts to predatory competition that works toward establishing one type of money, the best money.

At this point a very fundamental question arises: *How did money come about?* Menger argues in his treatise *Grundsätze der Volkswirthschaftslehre* (1871; *Principles of Economics*, 1994) that money developed solely on the basis of the self-interest of the people involved, and *spontaneously* in the free market, without the intervention of the state:

> The origin of money (as distinct from coin, which is only one variety of money) is, as we have seen, entirely natural.... Money is not an invention of the state. It is not the product of a legislative act. Even the sanction of political authority is not necessary for its existence. Certain commodities came to be money quite naturally, as the result of economic relationships that were independent of the power of the state.[36]

According to Menger, money arose from *material assets*, a commodity that, before it was used as money, was valued and traded solely for its non-monetary use. At some point it was used as money, because it was particularly suitable as a medium of exchange.

Menger's theory that money originated spontaneously from the free market, from a tangible asset, is subsequently confirmed by Ludwig von Mises in terms of the logic of action. With his *regression theorem*, Mises shows that Menger's theory of the formation of money is logically necessary.[37] Mises argues that money is in demand because it has purchasing power. The purchasing power of money is determined by the supply of and demand for money. But wait, isn't that *circular reasoning*? If you say that money is in demand because it has purchasing power, but at the same time you say that the purchasing power of money comes from the supply and demand for money—isn't the dog chasing its tail? The answer is no.

Mises shows that the demand for money has a *time dimension*. Money is in demand *today*, because it had purchasing power *yesterday*. And yesterday, money was in demand, because it had purchasing power

---

[36] Carl Menger, *Principles of Economics* trans. James Dingwall and Bert F. Hoselitz (1974; repr., Grove City, PA: Libertarian Press, 1994), pp. 261–62.

[37] It should only be pointed out here that the regression theorem applies a priori; it can be derived from the logic of human action.

the day before yesterday. And so on. If we go back further and further in time with this explanation, we finally arrive logically at the point at which a good was *first* used as money. At that time, the good must have already had a market price, which, however, was explained only by its *nonmonetary services*. This nonmonetary exchange value was the starting point for the first *purely monetary* exchange value of the good.

According to the regression theorem, it is therefore not possible to introduce money "from above." No ruler, no central authority can create money "just like that." This realization raises questions, above all, the question of how it can be that today's money is unbacked paper money. In his book *The Ethics of Money Production* (2008), the economist Jörg Guido Hülsmann writes pointedly: "Paper money has never been introduced through voluntary cooperation. In all known cases it has been introduced through coercion and compulsion, sometimes with the threat of the death penalty."[38] But if today's unbacked paper money cannot have originated "naturally" in the free market, how, then, did it enter the world? In order to find an answer to this question, it is necessary to first deal with the state. This is done in the following chapter.

[38] Jörg Guido Hülsmann, *The Ethics of Money Production* (Auburn, AL: Ludwig von Mises Institute, 2008), p. 172.

CHAPTER 7

THE DECIVILIZING FORCE: THE STATE

The State in and of itself is the most moral whole, the realization of freedom; and it is the absolute purpose of reason that freedom be real.

– **GEORG WILHELM FRIEDRICH HEGEL**

It is probably no exaggeration to say that most people regard the state (as we know it today) as indispensable: "Without it, nothing would work," it is often said. "Without the state, there would be neither law nor order; civilized coexistence would be impossible; all hell would be let loose." But careful reflection shows that this assessment *cannot* be correct. In order to understand this, one must first clarify what the state actually is.

The state is–in order to use a positive definition (i.e., an explanatory definition)–the territorial coercive monopolist with ultimate decision-making power. It is the entity which judges all conflicts or has the last word–that is, decides all conflicts that occur between its subordinates and also all conflicts that occur between its subordinates and itself. Every kindergarten child will immediately understand that no one would voluntarily give their consent to such a state. The question that arises here is: How can the state (as it has just been defined) have arisen?

It is logical that the state did not come into being on a voluntary basis. Among the living there will be no one who can truthfully claim that he was asked whether he wanted to be subjected to the state and who also agreed to it. Even the reference to the fact that the state came into existence by way of a *social contract* is not convincing. There is no such contract that you or I have ever signed. And anyone who then replies that the social contract which establishes the state is only a metaphor to symbolize the contractual concession, does not have a convincing argument either: he is merely trying (by coercion) to turn a yes into a no.

From the point of view of the logic of action, the state—if it is a territorial compulsory monopolist to which the individual is subjected for better or worse—is contradictory and thus literally wrong.[39] It de facto degrades the individual to a slave, and this is incompatible with the *logic of human action*—because property, self-ownership, is an indispensable category of human action. One cannot even argue without contradiction that the state is legitimate when people voluntarily submit to it. For then people are no longer owners of themselves and of the goods that they have acquired in a non-aggressive way.[40]

Of course, no one in his right mind would voluntarily and once and for all cede control over the welfare or suffering of himself and his property to the coercive monopolist which is the state, to a monopolist of all final decisions in his field, who has the power to unilaterally determine the extent and price of justice and security. Such a contract—if it existed—would simply be immoral. We cannot help but recognize that the existence of the today's state is the result of violence, conquest, oppression, and plunder. In this light Franz Oppenheimer (1864–1943)[41] writes:

> The State, completely in its genesis, essentially and almost completely during the first stages of its existence, is a social institution, forced by a victorious group of men onto a defeated group, with the sole purpose of regulating the dominion of the victorious group over the vanquished, and securing itself against revolt from within and attacks from abroad. Teleologically, this

[39] A well-known definition of logical contradiction can be found in George Orwell's dystopian novel *1984* (1949; Planet eBook, n.d.) in the form of *doublethink* (p. 197, italics in the original): "His mind slid away into the labyrinthine world of *doublethink*. To know and not to know, to be conscious of complete truthfulness while telling carefully constructed lies, to hold simultaneously two opinions which canceled out, knowing them to be contradictory and believing in both of them, to use logic against logic" (p. 198).

[40] As long as the individual voluntarily submits to the state, as long as he thinks and does what the state wants him to do, there seems to be no problem. But the problem becomes obvious if he does not want that, but something else. then the ugly face of the state appears, then the state forces him to obey. A taxation example: There are many people who say that they like to pay taxes, that they do not regard taxes as robbery because taxes are used for the benefit of society. But this doesn't justify their statement convincingly. The proof is in taking the liberty of denying the state taxes—and the reaction of the state will show the nature of taxes: violent expropriation, possibly associated with imprisonment or worse.

[41] Franz Oppenheimer was the doctoral supervisor of Ludwig Erhard (1897–1977), who admired him greatly.

dominion had no other purpose than the economic exploitation of the vanquished by the victors.[42]

It is often said that we need the state in order to protect property, and that without the state there would be no property at all. Is this argument convincing? The answer is no. Property must already have existed *before* the state—whose essence is the invasion of property—came into play. Property must have preceded the formation of the state. The state could only come into being *after* people had already created property. Obviously, you don't need the state to create property.

But can the aggression of the state against property perhaps be justified with the notion that without the state peaceful coexistence in the community would be impossible? This is a bee that Thomas Hobbes (1588–1679) put into his readers' bonnets when he wrote *Homo homini lupus est* ("Man is a wolf to man").[43] Let us suppose that Hobbes was right: *A* and *B*, in order to live peacefully together, needed a state *S*. Without *S*, *A* and *B* would live in anarchy; they would perish in conflict and struggle. They therefore have to ask for protection and security from *S* and from no other, and *S* alone determines what he charges them for it. In other words, *A* and *B* are subjected to *S*. The inalienable right of *A* and *B* to self-ownership is thus revoked.

But who now controls *S*, behind which people like *A* and *B* must necessarily hide? There is no reason why people who exercise the power of *S* should behave differently toward *A* and *B* than *A* and *B* behave toward each other. The logical conclusion would therefore be to control state *S* through a higher authority, state S^*. And S^* would again have to be controlled by S^{**}—and so on and so forth. Thought through consistently to the end, a world state would have to be established, to which all (*A* and *B* as well as *S*, S^*, S^{**}, and so on) are subjected. But who would control the world state? It is easy to see that this train of thought does not provide a convincing solution. The world state would also not be compatible with the a priori of property: like any nation-state, a world state could only emerge from aggression, from violence against the property of the individual.

We have realized that the state is an apparatus of violence. The question that now arises is: *How does such a state obtain its power*? It is well

---

[42] Franz Oppenheimer, *The State: Its History and Development Viewed Sociologically*, trans. John Gitterman (New York: B. W. Huebsch, 1922), p. 15.

[43] Hobbes's view has never been uncontroversial. While he sees the original urge of human action in the "egoistic" desire for self-preservation, Richard Cumberland (1631–1718), Samuel Pufendorf (1632–1694), and John Locke (1632–1704), for example, place it in "sociability."

known that a state can only survive as long as the subjects or governed—as a rule, they form the majority—do not rebel against the state or the rulers—as a rule, this is a small minority. The state can prevent such resistance in two ways. *First*, the state can force its existence by using naked force. After all, it has a monopoly on the use of force. However, this kind of power retention rests on clay feet and is also expensive. In addition, the state or its representatives must fear that they will be deposed by even more ruthless ones.

Second, it is far more effective for the state to form a *voluntary following*. This, in turn, can be achieved in three ways.

(1) The state dominates the educational system and spreads its self-glorifying ideology. To this end the state cooperates with intellectuals (teachers, professors, writers, actors, musicians, and artists), whom it pays and protects and ensures that they occupy public opinion in favor of the state. This obviously works very well: nowadays most people believe that the state is indispensable—and that reduces resistance against it.

(2) In principle, the state offers everyone the prospect (whether they have graduated school and college or not, whether they have rendered outstanding services to their fellow human beings or not) of being elected and thus coming to power if the individual so desires. This also makes the state an acceptable and supportive institution from the point of view of many—and also weakens the resistance against it.

(3) The state blatantly corrupts people. It proverbially buys the support of the electorate by promising them privileges and incomes that they would not be able to obtain through their own work. The state therefore acts according to the principle of *divide et impera*: divide and rule.

Many people quickly recognize the state as an appropriate means to achieve their personal goals: all that is needed are ruling parties that are empowered to implement and enforce what is desired.[44] This means that sooner or later everything and everyone will be politicized: state influence is spreading to all areas of society and life—education, work, health, pensions, the environment, food, transport, security, legislative, judicial, money, and credit—and the state is becoming the dominant player everywhere.

[44] It is precisely small and well-organized interest groups that influence state legislation and regulation effectively in their favor, as Mancur Olson (1932–98) explains in *The Logic of Collective Action: Public Goods and the Theory of Groups* (Cambridge, MA: Harvard University Press, 1965).

The French economist and thinker Claude-Frédéric Bastiat (1801-1850) finds clear words to this effect:

> The state is the great fictitious entity by which everyone seeks to live at the expense of everyone else. For, today as in the past, each of us, more or less, would like to profit from the labor of others. One does not dare to proclaim this feeling publicly, one conceals it from oneself, and then what does one do? One imagines an intermediary; one addresses the state, and each class proceeds in turn to say to it: "You, who can take fairly and honorably, take from the public and share with us." Alas! The state is only too ready to follow such diabolical advice; for it is composed of cabinet ministers, of bureaucrats, of men, in short, who, like all men, carry in their hearts the desire, and always enthusiastically seize the opportunity, to see their wealth and influence grow. The state understands, then, very quickly the use it can make of the role the public entrusts to it. It will be the arbiter, the master, of all destinies. It will take a great deal; hence, a great deal will remain for itself. It will multiply the number of its agents; it will enlarge the scope of its prerogatives; it will end by acquiring over-whelming proportions.[45]

Bastiat's reference to the fact that the state cannot be limited deserves special attention. Indeed, anyone who hopes that the expansion of the state can be effectively contained by constitutional rules is hoping in vain. The state also monopolizes legislation and jurisprudence. Thus, it makes itself the judge of all conflicts, including those that it itself has started. It is obvious that under these conditions, case law is in favor of the state (especially in questions of existential importance to it). After all, the courts are staffed and paid by the state. The judiciary may emancipate itself from the influence of the ruling party which currently has power and authority, but not from the state itself.

We cannot help but reach this conclusion: the creation and continued existence of the state are not based on voluntarism, but on violence and coercion. Of course, there are states that abuse their (coercive) monopoly more than others; from this point of view, we could speak of "bad" and

---

[45] Claude-Frédéric Bastiat, *Selected Essays on Political Economy*, trans. Seymour Cain and ed. George B. de Huszar (Irvington-on-Hudson, NY: Foundation for Economic Education, 1995), p. 144.

"less bad" states. But they all constitute a violation of property rights. States are, as Hoppe puts it, expropriating property protectors and law-breaking law-keepers—and thereby release decivilizing forces. The modern democratic state especially is continuing to expand. Attempts to tame and enclose it prove to be an illusion. *Even a minimal state becomes a maximal state sooner or later.*[46] This logical insight has a counterpart in reality.

Wherever you look: in recent decades, states have become increasingly powerful, and they have spared no area of economic and social life. Above all, states claim the monopoly of money production. The reason for this is that once the state has gained sovereignty over money, the path is clear for the greatest possible expansion of power: the state can then literally buy everything and everyone. It is therefore no coincidence that states now have a monopoly on money all over the world. Chapter 8 examines the steps by which they have gradually gained control over money, sometimes through intricate paths.

[46] According to Hans-Hermann Hoppe, *Democracy: The God That Failed: The Economics and Politics of Monarchy, Democracy, and Natural Order* (New Brunswick, NJ: Transaction Publishers, 2006), p. 229.

CHAPTER 8

THE STATE AND THE DETERIORATION OF MONEY: FROM COMMODITY MONEY TO FIAT MONEY

[H]istory ... provides the most vivid illustration of the direct link between a state's internal powers of counterfeiting and its policy of external aggression, as well as the banking and business elite's conspiracy with the state in its expansionary desires.

– **HANS-HERMANN HOPPE**

The state has only *one* source of finance: the income and assets of its subjects. But how can the state acquire these funds? It can rob openly by levying *taxes*. But that quickly reaches its limits. The robbed realize that they are being looted and rebel if they feel the tax burden is too high. It is much more convenient for the state if it can create *money* at its own discretion and buy the desired goods and services on the market in return. But how does the state find such a favorable position for itself?

As shown in chapter 6, money can only come from a tangible asset. Even a state cannot create money simply by decree. If the state wants to become the absolute ruler of money, it must first make do with what is there already: commodity money in the form of gold and silver.[47] To gain full sovereignty over money, the state must work over the long term. As a first step, it will monopolize the *coin business*: coins may be minted from

[47] For this explanation see Murray N. Rothbard, *What Has Government Done to Our Money?*, 5th ed. (Auburn, AL: Ludwig von Mises Institute, 2010).

now on only in the national mint. A fee is charged for minting gold and silver coins. The mint profit (seigniorage) goes to the state.

The coins are given the state stamp, a symbol that is acceptable to the state. The state will ensure that the name of the coin is separated from its physical material. For example, "gold gram" or "silver ounce" become "US dollar," "mark," or "franc." In this way, the commodity money in circulation is most closely linked to the ruler or the state.

Once the state has the monopoly over the minting of coins, it sets about reducing the precious metal content of the coins. Put simply: one mark, which previously equaled 0.50 grams of fine gold, now contains only 0.25 grams of fine gold. This allows the outstanding amount of money that can be extracted from a given stock of precious metals to be increased (in this case doubled). The state earns by reducing the precious metal fineness of the coins. But such a *coin debasement* quickly reaches its limits: if the coins literally become too light, the fraud is noticeable and the acceptance of the coins in trade dwindles. The state will therefore look for more effective measures.

In a *commodity money system*, the state can take a major step toward its objective of enriching itself by allowing banks to operate with a fractional reserve. In other words, it allows banks to create their own money by granting loans: banks issue banknotes and sight deposits on credit that exceed the amount of gold and silver that customers have stored with them. The increase of money by credit serves the interests of the state and the banks. The state can borrow from the banks and pays an interest rate that is lower than the interest that would normally have to be paid. The banks benefit because lending in a fractional reserve system gives them high profits.

But there's a catch: if customers realize that banks can't convert *all* the banknotes and bank balances they've issued into precious metal at any time, as they promised, panic can easily break out. Then the customers storm the bank counters (bank run) and demand the exchange of their banknotes and sight deposits for precious metal. If the banks are unable to do so in full, their insolvency becomes apparent. If one bank fails in a fractional reserve system, it is very likely that all other banks will also become insolvent.

Consequently, if a bank run occurs in a fractional reserve system, the state uses a trick: it suspends the banks' obligation to in redeem precious metals. Owners of banknotes and sight deposits will be informed that their claims will no longer be exchangeable for gold, at least temporarily. Such a suspension of the gold redeemability of banknotes and sight deposits is, however, awkward for the state and banks. Those affected, who no longer have access to their gold, protest, and the trick cannot be repeated too often. Suspending the promise to exchange bank money for gold is therefore not a satisfactory solution for the state and the banks.

For them it is much more advantageous if the money is dematerialized and thus can be multiplied at will, and if there is a central authority that directs the fate of the dematerialized money—in favor of the state and the banks. In other words, the state and banks want a *central bank* that has a monopoly on money production. Such a central bank, which enjoys great prestige and trust—after all, the state stands behind it—reduces the likelihood of a bank run, and thus increases the inflationary potential of the state and the banks.

With a central bank, the backing of money by gold can be ended. And this is exactly what in the meantime has happened in all countries of the world. It has taken a long time to get there. But in the end the states were successful: they have gained the monopoly over money production and replaced the material, or gold, money with their own *unbacked paper money*. Let us look at the example of the United States. The Coin Act of 1792 defines the US dollar in gold and silver fine weights.[48] The United States thus has a *bimetallic system*: gold and silver are officially money. In 1873, silver is demonetized, and the dollar is de facto defined only in gold. From now on, $20.67 equals one troy ounce of gold.

On April 5, 1933, President Franklin D. Roosevelt (1882–1945) bans Americans from owning gold. The gold stocks stored in banks must be handed over to the US Treasury Department. In return, customers receive dollar banknotes and sight deposits at US banks. Americans will no longer be able to exchange their banknotes or bank deposits for physical gold. The yellow metal disappears from daily payment transactions. Only large-volume, international payment transactions between central banks are carried out with gold.

---

[48] 371.25 grains of fine silver and 24.75 grains of fine gold equaled $1; 1 troy ounce of gold (31.10347 grams) equaled 480 grains. Because the dollar was defined as 371.25 grains of silver, 1 troy ounce of silver was about $1.2929 (480 grains divided by 371.25 grains per troy ounce), and the price of 1 troy ounce of gold was about $19.3939 (480 divided by 24.75). See also Milton Friedman, *Money Mischief: Episodes in Monetary History* (San Diego, CA: Hartcourt Brace, 1994), pp. 53ff.

In early 1934, the Roosevelt administration decide to *devalue* the dollar against gold (the Gold Reserve Act). For that purpose, the previous price of gold is raised from $20.67 to $35 per troy ounce. As a result, gold rises by 69 percent against the dollar—and accordingly the purchasing power of the US dollar, measured in gold, drops by about 41 percent. Since this measure increased the amount of dollar money, goods prices subsequently also rose markedly. By the way, it was more than forty years before President Gerald Ford (1913–2006) decided in August 1974 to lift the gold ban: it was not until 1975 that Americans were allowed to own gold again.

But gold does not lose its money status as a result. In 1944, an agreement is reached in the form of the *Bretton Woods system* to restructure the world's monetary relations.[49] The US dollar is chosen as the world reserve currency. Thirty-five dollars is equivalent to one troy ounce of gold. The other currencies (such as the British pound and the French franc) are pegged to the dollar at a fixed exchange rate. Thus, they are indirectly anchored to gold. However, we should not jump to the conclusion that the Bretton Woods system was a gold standard. It was only a pseudo-gold standard;[50] chapter 16 explains this in more detail.

The Bretton Woods system fails due to its faulty design. On August 15, 1971, President Richard Nixon (1913–1994) proclaims that the gold redeemability of the US dollar is *temporarily* suspended; this is the largest act of monetary expropriation in currency history. As a result of this unilateral decision by the Americans, the US dollar and all other important currencies of the world are deprived of their gold cover. Thus the world monetary system loses its anchorage in gold. The currencies are turned into fiat money by a *coup de main*. The following chapter explains in more detail what fiat money is and what it causes.

---

[49] See for example Ben Steil, *The Battle of Bretton Woods: John Maynard Keynes, Harry Dexter White, and the Making of a New World Order* (Princeton, NJ: Princeton University Press, 2013).

[50] See also Thorsten Polleit and Michael von Prollius, *Geldreform: Vom schlechten Staatsgeld zum guten Marktgeld* (Munich: FinanzBuch Verlag, 2014), pp. 247ff.

CHAPTER 9

ANATOMY OF A DISRUPTION: WHAT FIAT MONEY CAUSES

Paper money appears at first sight to be a great saving, or rather that it costs nothing; but it is the dearest money there is.[51]

– **THOMAS PAINE**

The word *fiat* comes from Latin and its meaning amounts to "it shall be" or "let it be done." Fiat money is not "natural money" in the sense that it could have been created in the free market by voluntary agreement between market players. We can call fiat money–according to the saying "sink or swim"–a *coerced* money, a *decreed* money. (With tongue in cheek one could say: If you are forced to call a dog a cat and treat it like one, then the dog is a *fiat* cat.)

Fiat money has three characteristics: (1) Fiat money is state-monopolized money; the state central banks control the production of money. (2) Fiat money is usually created through lending, which is not matched by real savings.[52] It is created "out of nothing" (or *ex nihilo* in Latin). (3) Fiat money is dematerialized money. It has the form of colorfully printed paper slips (more precisely, pieces of cotton) and entries on computer files (bits and bytes). Whether US dollars, euros, Chinese renminbi, Japanese yen, British pounds, or Swiss francs, they are all fiat money.

Because fiat money is not a *natural*, free market money–it is not the result of voluntary exchanges–it is not surprising that it suffers from severe economic and ethical deficits. Fiat money is *inflationary*: it loses

[51] Thomas Paine, *Dissertations on Government, the Affairs of the Bank, and Paper Money* (Philadelphia: Charles Cist, 1838), p. 52.

[52] Fiat money can also be created by, for example, the central bank printing new money to pay its employees.

its purchasing power over time, because the central banks—in close cooperation with the commercial banks—are continually expanding the supply of fiat money. And if the money supply rises, so do the prices of goods, and this necessarily lowers the purchasing power of money.

Inflation, by the way, can occur with commodity money as well as for fiat money. But because a fiat money supply can be expanded at any time to the politically desired amount, fiat money is much more inflationary than commodity money; and that is also the reason why the state has replaced commodity money with its own fiat money.

The chronic inflation of fiat money ensures that income and wealth *are redistributed in a way that does not conform to market conditions*, with the first recipients of the newly created money benefiting at the expense of the late recipients. Those who are the first to receive the newly created money can purchase goods at unchanged prices. If the new money spreads through the economy, the prices of goods will rise—or they will be higher compared to a situation in which the money supply had not been increased. The redistributive effect—some getting richer at the expense of many—necessarily occurs, because not all people participate at the increase of the quantity of fiat money.[53]

As the purchasing power of fiat money melts away over time, savers have no choice but to go to the bank to set up interest-bearing deposits and securities accounts in the hope of earning an interest yield that will protect them from the decline in monetary value. Fiat money thus immensely increases the business and profit opportunities of the banking and financial industry—after all, the customer has to pay fees for accounts, deposits, and transactions. It is therefore anything but surprising that the banking and financial sector in particular is a fervent supporter of the fiat money system!

By putting new money into circulation, preferably through loans that are not covered by real savings, the central bank artificially lowers the market interest rate. The central bank thereby causes a large-scale deception: consumers and entrepreneurs are deluded by an illusion of wealth. They are misled about the true conditions of scarcity; their decisions on consumption, savings, and investment become misguided. This causes serious disturbances in the economic and financial fabric.

---

[53] See Ludwig von Mises, *The Theory of Money and Credit*, trans. by J. E. Batson (New Haven, CT: Yale University Press, 1953), pp. 139–43.

The artificially lowered market interest rate tempts people to save less and consume more, and at the same time motivates companies to make new investments. As a result, the economy lives beyond its means. But this is not apparent at first, because the artificially lowered interest rate sets an *artificial* upswing (boom) in motion. It ensures that corporate profits bubble up, employment increases and wages rise. But the boom is built on sand: after the one-off injection of the new fiat money has had an impact on commodity prices and wages, companies notice that the increased demand for their products was a one-off and not permanent and that their profits are lagging behind expectations.

Investment projects that have been started but not yet completed are then liquidated and reversed. Jobs previously created will be cut and workers' wages and incomes will fall again. The boom turns into a downturn (bust). The banks in particular contribute to this: the loans that they have granted to consumers and companies are either in default of payment or are canceled. The banks then become more cautious about lending, reducing their risk appetite. The result: the influx of new loans and new fiat money into the economic system dries up.

The market interest rate then begins to rise again, and the economy returns to its original savings-consumption-investment ratio—to the situation that was preferred by market participants before the artificial lowering of the market interest rate, to a situation in which more was saved, less consumed, and less invested than in the artificial boom. But as a result, the boom collapses—and with it the production and employment structure that has developed as a result of artificially lowered interest rates. The result is an economic and financial crisis.

The bust may be painful, but it is economically necessary. It corrects the economic damage caused by the boom: overconsumption and bad investments. The bust ensures that production and employment are adapted back to the actual needs of the customer. But the bust is politically unpopular: Who wants to accept a loss of income, be driven out of traditional markets, forgo accustomed achievements, who wants to have to admit mistakes? Hardly anyone! And so, when the boom threatens to turn into a bust, the public call for cuts in interest rates is loud.

Even lower interest rates are supposed to turn the bust into another boom. The central bank responds to the request—and the game begins all over again. This explains the cycle of boom and bust. However, the damage caused by the distortion of interest rates by the central banks is not yet fully described. The artificially low interest rate upgrades current consumption compared to future consumption. The consequences of this *value manipulation* can be seen in many ways. For example, interest rate cuts by central banks drive up prices and valuation levels for equities, land, and buildings.[54] Mind you, such price increases are the symptoms of one cause—the change in people's values due to interest rate policy. But interest rate manipulation by central banks has much more far-reaching effects.

The central banks artificially drive people's time preferences up by manipulating market interest rates downwards.[55] When interest rates are artificially lowered, it becomes more important for people to achieve short-term goals compared to long-term goals. Interest rate reduction, for example, encourages a life on credit, i.e., to bring forward consumption opportunities at the expense of the future. Saving goes out of fashion, permanent debt becomes morally acceptable. And when the present and immediate becomes more and more important, the willingness to achieve also decreases: people prefer to work less, because leisure time becomes more important (more about this in chapter 20).

Above all, however, the boom-and-bust cycles for which central bank policies are responsible do most people great harm: they suffer job losses, become socially dependent, and lose their old-age provision. They attribute the cause of their suffering to the free market economy—but not to the state fiat money system. (This erroneous interpretation of the cause of the crisis is provided by the many economists on the state's payroll, who publicly blame the free markets and not the state!) Entrepreneurs and workers call for even more state intervention in the market to improve the economic situation. This includes in particular the call for even lower interest rates.

Mises expresses this tragedy:

> Nothing harmed the cause of liberalism more than the almost regular return of feverish booms and of the dramatic breakdown of bull markets followed by lingering slumps. Public opinion has become convinced that such happenings are inevitable in the unhampered market economy. People did not conceive that what they lamented was the necessary outcome of policies directed toward a lowering of the rate of interest by

---

[54] Stated simply: if market interest rates fall, this drives up the present values of discounted future payments—and thus also their market prices.

[55] See Thorsten Polleit, *A Brief Note on Bank Circulation Credit and Time Preference* (Place: Publisher, forthcoming).

means of credit expansion. They stubbornly kept to these policies and tried in vain to fight their undesired consequences by more and more government interference.[56]

And further:

The boom produces impoverishment. But still more disastrous are its moral ravages. It makes people despondent and dispirited. The more optimistic they were under the illusory prosperity of the boom, the greater is their despair and their feeling of frustration. The individual is always ready to ascribe his good luck to his own efficiency and to take it as a well-deserved reward for his talent, application, and probity. But reverses of fortune he always charges to other people, and most of all to the absurdity of social and political institutions. He does not blame the authorities for having fostered the boom. He reviles them for the necessary collapse. In the opinion of the public, more inflation and more credit expansion are the only remedy against the evils which inflation and credit expansion have brought about.[57]

The central problem of fiat money is this: the economies get into *debt bondage*. The ever-increasing debt in the fiat monetary system increases the dependence on the continuation of the low interest rate policy not only for debtors, but also for savers, investors, and the entire production and employment structure. Companies, employees, and government representatives do not want to fail, do not want their debt to end in a large-scale default and a major crisis. In other words, something like "collective corruption"[58] emerges.

People become economically and socially dependent on the continuation of the fiat money system. Therefore, it is not surprising that they, in their own interests, advocate measures that maintain the fiat monetary system and the structures it has created and prevent them from collapsing, even if it means dismantling what is left of the free market economy. No wonder that the preferred measure is the policy of interest rate cuts and to expand the supply of credit and money.[59]

---

[56] Mises, *Human Action*, p. 441.

[57] Ibid., p. 574.

[58] See Thorsten Polleit, "Fiat Money and Collective Corrupton," *Quarterly Journal of Austrian Economics* 14, no. 4 (Winter 2011): 397–415

[59] See Fritz Machlup, *Führer durch die Krisenpolitik*, vol. 6 of *Beiträge zur Konjunkturforschung* (Vienna: Verlag Julius Springer, 1934), pp. 41–44.

But this only prolongs the crisis, thereby making it bigger. In the words of Ludwig von Mises:

> The wavelike movement affecting the economic system, the recurrence of periods of boom which are followed by periods of depression, is the unavoidable outcome of the attempts, repeated again and again, to lower the gross market rate of interest by means of credit expansion. There is no means of avoiding the final collapse of a boom brought about by credit expansion. The alternative is only whether the crisis should come sooner as the result of a voluntary abandonment of further credit expansion, or later as a final and total catastrophe of the currency system involved.[60]

It is far from surprising that states that claim to be welfare states insist on their monopoly of money production. The welfare state is a wolf in sheep's clothing, a deceptive package. Its supporters—little by little and often by stealth—try to use it to realize their socialist dreams in economy and society. Behind the talked-up idea of the welfare state lies an *ideological program hostile to freedom*—and it bears the name of *democratic socialism.* The following chapter is dedicated to it.

ABOUT THE MARKET INTEREST RATE AND ORIGINAL INTEREST RATE

What is interest? In order to explain the phenomenon of interest, it makes sense to first distinguish between *market interest* rates and *originary interest* rates. The market interest rate is formed by the supply of and demand for savings (used for investment purposes) on the market. In the simplest case, it consists of individual components. These include inflation and risk premiums as well as the so-called *originary interest rate.*

Originary interest is the result of *time preference.* It is a category of human action and is explained as follows: action takes *time*; timeless action cannot be conceptualized without contradictions. Time is therefore a *means* of achieving objectives and, like any means, time is *scarce.* Consequently, the actor values the fulfillment of a need in

[60] Mises, *Human Action*, p. 570.

the present *more highly* than the fulfillment of the need (of the same nature and otherwise under the same conditions) at a later date.

If an actor has an originary interest rate of, say, 2 percent, he will only be prepared to exchange 1 euro, which he owns today for 1.02 euros which he will receive in one year. If he were to receive only, say, 1.01 euros in a year for his current 1 euro, there would be no exchange of "euro today" for "euro in a year"; and there would be no market interest rate either.

Time preference and originary interest differ from person to person, and these can change over time. For example, they can move in the direction of the zero line. But time preference and the originary interest rate can never become zero or negative; they cannot be ignored in people's values and actions. This statement is not based on any arbitrary (behavioral) assumption but follows from the logic of *human action*.[61]

Let's take the position of the devil's advocate at this point and think through what it means if the originary interest rate in the economy actually falls to zero: if your personal originary interest rate, dear reader, were 0 percent (if you had no time preference), then you would prefer two apples, which you will only get in ten years or in one thousand years, rather than one apple today. If your originary interest rate were zero, then only "more is better than less" means anything to you, whereas "sooner is better than later" has no meaning for your values and actions.

An originary interest rate of 0 percent would drive the land prices, which result from the discounting of all future land rents to the present, to infinity. Plots of land would be priceless! Anyone who says that the originary interest is zero implicitly denies that resources

[61] This can be explained with the logical final figure of the *modus (tollendo) tollens*: an accepted conditional statement is "If p, then q." Assuming we observe (or say) "not q," we conclude that the antecedent is negated, i.e., "not p." Let us assume that *p* stands for the statement "Humans act" and *q* for the statement "The originary interest rate is always and everywhere positive." If we say, "not q" (i.e., "The originary interest rate is *not* always and everywhere positive"), then "not p" must apply (i.e., "Humans *cannot* act"). Here, however, "not-p" is (praxeo-)logically wrong: one cannot deny the sentence "Humans act" without contradiction. Anyone who says, "Humans do *not* act," has acted himself and thus contradicts what has been said. For the *modus tollendo tollens* see Morris R. Cohen and Ernest Nagel, *An Introduction to Logic and Scientific Method* (1934; repr., New York: Simon Publications, 2002), pp. 101–05.

are scarce—and that can be seen as logically wrong.[62] It would mean that you would no longer consume anything of your income, and save and invest everything in order to enjoy more goods: you do not consume today, not tomorrow, not in one year, not in ten years. A completely absurd idea! And a negative originary interest rate is not at all meaningfully conceivable for human logic!

The many examples that mainstream economists offer to justify a negative originary interest rate cannot refute what has been said above. If, for example, the gold market is in *contango* (i.e., the forward price exceeds the spot price), this does not mean that time preference and the originary interest rates of the market participants are negative. And neither are both negative even if the price you are willing to pay for ice cream next summer is higher than it is today, in winter. In these examples, in addition to the originary interest rate (which is always and everywhere positive), there is another factor in determining value which takes into account the conditions of action at the time when action is taken; this was pointed out by the US economist Frank A. Fetter (1863–1949).

In "pure form," the originary interest rate *only* appears in the exchange of a currently available monetary unit for a monetary unit that will only be available in the future, but not in the intertemporal exchange of *material goods*. There may be pensioners who feel well provided for today and for whom future goods provision is more important than in the present. But even then, these pensioners value a monetary unit that is available today higher than the monetary unit that will only be available in the future: they value one euro today higher than one euro (and of course also 0.95 euros) in ten years. The originary interest rate even of these pensioners is positive; for logical reasons it cannot be zero or negative.

---

[62] The assumption of an originary interest rate of zero implies that there is no scarcity in the field of human action—and that is a logical contradiction. See Mises, *Nationalökonomie*, pp. 479ff.; also Jeffrey M. Herbener, Comment on "A Note on Two Erroneous Ways of Defending the PTPT of Interest," *Quarterly Journal of Austrian Economics* 16, no. 3 (Fall 2013): 317–30, esp. 322ff.

CHAPTER 10

A DESTRUCTIVE IDEOLOGY: DEMOCRATIC SOCIALISM

In socialist ideas, the most daring idealism has always met the most covetous materialism.
— **HEINRICH VON TREITSCHKE**

Socialism promises people a better world with enticing words: a world where peace reigns, where justice and good fortune prevail. Economically, socialism entails that the means of production are not privately owned, but nationalized, i.e., owned by the state. As an economic and social model, socialism is thus the opposite of *capitalism*, which describes the economic and social model in which the means of production are privately owned. But, however tempting its promises may sound, socialism is not feasible.

The impossibility of socialism was conclusively explained, using scientific means, by Ludwig von Mises in 1919 in his essay "Die Wirtschaftsrechnung im sozialistischen Gemeinwesen" ("Economic Calculation in the Socialist Commonwealth"). In short, under socialism—because there is no ownership of the means of production—there can be no market prices for scarce goods. Without them, however, an economic calculation is completely impossible. The socialist planners cannot know in which quantity and quality, goods are desired, nor can they assess the feasibility of production projects. Socialism leads to chaos, violence and impoverishment—as opposed to all contrary proclamations of salvation.[63]

[63] Even the worst experiences with socialism—think of Stalin, Hitler, Mao Zedong, Pol Pot—are not enough to discredit it once and for all. This is mainly due to the following reason: In the field of human action, of human history, experience can never provide the convincing and conclusive proof that something had to proceed as it did. The history of human action always forms a complex of many individual phenomena, whose respective influence on the final result can never be determined separately. Therefore, no laws can be derived from human history, the way they

To be sure, socialism comes in different forms and manifestations.[64] But there are two basic forms that can be distinguished. On the one hand, there is the *socialism of Russian influence* (also called: *Marxism-Leninism*). It stands for revolution and bloody overthrow, for the violent expropriation of the owners and the nationalization of the means of production. On the other hand there is the *socialism of German influence*: German socialists recognized that the Russian path to socialism could not be implemented in Germany. It was too ruthless, too cruel to have any prospect of success in Germany. The German socialists therefore opted for a different strategy. They were in favor of retaining in principle the private ownership of the means of production. At the same time, however, they demanded that the owners should not be entitled to all the revenue they generated by the use of their property. Part of it belonged to the community and was to be paid to the state in the form of taxes.

Once the democratic socialists have found support for their demands, the way ahead is virtually preprogrammed. If one has regarded partial expropriation as correct and good, then no principled reason can be raised any more against ever further tax increases. If an initial income tax of, say, 20 percent is levied, then over time it will become 25, 30, 35, 40 percent, or more. These small steps lead to the progressive expropriation of income earners and to an ever-greater redistribution of income and wealth based on political considerations, which increases the power of the state and the groups it favors. Private property then exists only formally, but no longer in economic terms. Thus, from the point of view of democratic socialism, property is *property by grace of the state*; it is *fiat property*.

Democratic socialism finds its intellectual basis in *cultural Marxism* (or *neo-Marxism*). It has grown out of the Marxist-Leninist insight that the hoped-for revolution does not emanate from the working masses, but

are gleaned from scientific investigations (here, the isolated influence of a factor on the final result can usually be filtered out by means of laboratory experiments). Consequently, a theory concerning human action, such as socialism, cannot be confirmed as true or refuted as false by experience. It is precisely this insight that the socialists make active use of. They explain that socialism, where and when it was put into practice, did not produce the hoped-for results, with the following: socialism had not been implemented consistently enough. At the next attempt one must proceed more resolutely—and then it will be obvious that socialism works. Or the next time, all that needs to be done is to place more capable people at the levers of socialism, and they will lead socialism to victory and, as promised, create a fairer and more peaceful world in no time. Many other subterfuges and attempts at justification could be cited to excuse the failure of socialism and the horrors it brings to people. On the history of socialism see Erik von Kuehnelt-Leddihn, *Leftism Revisited: From de Sade and Marx to Hitler and Pol Pot* (Washington, DC: Regnery Gateway, 1990), pp. 33ff.

[64] See Ludwig von Mises, *Die Gemeinwirtschaft: Untersuchungen über den Sozialismus* (Stuttgart: Lucius und Lucius, 1932), esp. pp. 56–61.

that instead the basis for the transformation of society must be created by the intellectuals. The goal is not sudden violent overthrow, but a creeping peaceful upheaval—through the change of values, culture, and beliefs of the people. In this way, the masses, denuded of meaning and disoriented, are ultimately to effectively fall into the clutches of communism.

After decades of persistent preparatory work (the "march through the institutions"), cultural Marxist intellectuals today occupy many key positions in politics, administration, art, and culture. They can be found especially in schools and universities, popularizing their ideas, which are veiled in the garb of democratic socialism. New group conflicts are constantly being stirred up and talked up—whether it is a question of gender or nationality—which unsettle people and deliberately confuse them, until emotions reach psychotic proportions.

Political globalism relies on democratic socialism. Its aim is to direct and determine in an authoritarian way all relations between people from different continents. According to them, it is not the free market, the division of labor, and free trade that should determine what is produced and consumed when and where, but rather these decisions should be influenced or made by an ideological and political creative will. Political globalism receives support not only from the political left. Large companies in particular are expressing their support—because they hope to be able to influence the political process in their favor.[65]

Democratic socialism has—and this can be shown with the *a priori* theory of action—negative consequences for the material prosperity and morality of society. Here are a few examples. Taxing company profits reduces the return on investment: it is lower compared to a situation in which entrepreneurs are not taxed. This makes investing less attractive. The capital stock is growing less strongly than it actually could, and consequently future real wage increases will be lower than they would otherwise be.

The incentive to work, to engage in productive activity, decreases because the cost of not working decreases. Under democratic socialism, one can ultimately earn (transfer) income without having to offer a marketable service. All you have to do is elect a government to power that will give you the desired benefits. The bill has to be paid by the taxpayers, the productive people—who then have a reduced incentive to be productive.

[65] See Thorsten Polleit, "Bewahrt die wirtschaftliche Globalisierung: Freihandel und Polit-Globalismus sind nicht das gleiche," *Schweizerzeit*, Jan. 27, 2017.

The material prosperity of the economy as a whole will therefore be lower compared to a situation where there is no taxation.

Democratic socialism abolishes the sharp distinction between "mine" and "yours." Anyone who is allowed to vote for a government will vote for the party he expects will improve his financial situation, even if that happens at the expense of his fellow human beings. In order to defend themselves, actual and potential victims of the election results (the productive ones, whom one can take things away from) will also want to get politically involved. This leads to a politicization of the community that encompasses all areas of life, from which nothing and nobody is spared. The "political struggle" that ensues increasingly diverts scarce resources (money, time, personnel, etc.) from productive to unproductive uses.

Above all, however, democratic socialism ruins social morality. In a free market economy, you can only earn and preserve income and wealth if you do something that others demand voluntarily. You have to consistently place your labor at the service of customer wishes and prove yourself anew every day. In a free market economy, income and wealth are therefore the reward for serving one's fellow human beings.

In democratic socialism a different moral and value concept emerges. In democratic socialism, unlike in a free market economy, there is less incentive to earn an income and build wealth by aligning one's abilities with the desires of fellow human beings. Above all, there is no longer any unconditional respect for the property of others. Their income and assets are instead downgraded to potential prey, which can be appropriated with impunity if one elects the appropriate party, the idea being: *The government takes something away from the others, and it gives me a bit of the loot.* Democratic socialism thus creates a permanent conflict by dividing the community into *net state profiteers* and *net state losers.*

Democratic socialism, however, faces a particularly sensitive problem when it is spatially limited: In a single region, the policy of taxation and redistribution of income and wealth is more or less limited as long as there is an international free movement of labor and capital. For example, if companies and workers are taxed very heavily in the country where democratic socialism prevails, they migrate to other countries where the tax burden is comparatively lower. This is a thorn in the side of the democratic socialists.

The emigration of productive people ultimately reduces the available volume of taxation and redistribution that the democratic socialists can seize. Democratic socialism can only get the problem of "voting with one's feet" under control if it succeeds in establishing global democratic socialism under a unified leadership. But how can that succeed? This question will be examined in more detail in the following chapters. Before that, however, it will be shown how a priori theory can help to better understand and estimate the developmental dynamics of democratic socialism and its socio-economic consequences.

CHAPTER 11

IMPACT ASSESSMENT: A CASE FOR THE A PRIORI THEORY

Man is so intelligent that he feels impelled to invent theories to account for what happens in the world. Unfortunately, he is not quite intelligent enough, in most cases, to find correct explanations. So that when he acts on his theories, he behaves very often like a lunatic.[66]

– **ALDOUS HUXLEY**

Chapter four highlighted the role of a priori theory for interpreting historical events meaningfully. But a priori theory has another field of application: it enables a *future-oriented assessment of the consequences of action*. However, let us immediately prevent a possible misunderstanding: this does not mean that a priori theory can be used to predict how people will behave in the future (which products they will ask for, how they will react to technical changes, which parties they will vote for, etc.). Not at all!

Human action cannot be predicted in the same way predictions are made in the natural sciences. In the natural sciences, quantifiable cause-and-effect relationships such as "If *A*, then *B*" or "If *A* increases by *x* percent, *B* changes by *y* percent" can be explored. Such "regularities" cannot be found in the area of human action, there is *no constancy of behavior* here. Different people react differently to the same influencing factor at different times. This is not an arbitrary assertion, but a logical conclusion derived from the undeniable ability of human beings to learn.

[66] Aldous Huxley, *Texts and Pretexts: An Anthology with Commentaries* (New York: Harper and Brothers Publishers, 1933), p. 278.

The statement that people are capable of learning cannot be denied without contradiction:[67] (1) Anyone who argues that humans are not capable of learning presupposes that others do not yet know the content of what he is saying that they are therefore capable of learning (otherwise he would not say what he is saying). He therefore commits a *performative contradiction.* (2) When someone says, "Humans can learn that they cannot learn," he assumes that he learned at some point that humans cannot learn, thereby attesting to the ability to learn. He is committing an *open contradiction.* Consequently, for logical reasons we cannot deny the ability to learn; it exists a priori.

However, the ability to learn now implies that external factors (physical, chemical, or biological) cannot systematically explain or predict human actions (in the sense of a cause-and-effect relationship)—otherwise we could know today how people will act in the future: future behavior could be predicted by looking at current conditions, and we would already know today how people will behave in the future. The actors would then already know today everything they could ever know in the future. But that would mean that they could no longer act, no longer influence the course of things; they will have been degraded to a kind of automaton. Not only does this sound absurd, but it is absurd: it cannot be conceived logically without contradiction because of the ability to learn, which cannot be denied.

We know with a priori certainty which implications the sentence "Humans act" include, these can be determined by consistent thinking. What we cannot know or predict with certainty, however, is *how* people will act in the future, how they will react to certain influencing factors, and what the conditions will be under which action will be taken;[68] the Polish sociologist Stanislav Andreski (1919–2007) stresses that "it is logically impossible for anyone to ever understand his own mind and thus be able to make exact predictions about its future conditions."[69]

Therefore, the question arises: Can a priori theory shed any light on what *might happen in the future*? The answer is yes, it can, albeit only within very narrow limits: the a priori logic of action makes it possible

[67] See Hans-Hermann Hoppe, *Kritik der kausalwissenschaftlichen Sozialforschung: Untersuchungen zur Grundlegung von Soziologie und Ökonomie* (Opladen, Germany: Westdeutscher Verlag, 1983), pp. 11–15, 25–29, 44–49 and here chap. 3.

[68] On the limits of future knowledge, see Holm Tetens, *Wissenschaftstheorie: Eine Einführung* (Munich: C. H. Beck, 2013), pp. 94ff.

[69] Stanislav Andreski, *Die Hexenmeister der Sozialwissenschaften: Mißbrauch, Mode und Manipulationen einer Wissenschaft* (Munich: List Verlag, 1974), p. 16.

to reliably identify the necessary qualitative (but not quantitative) consequences and sequences of human action that take place under certain conditions.

An example: the current situation does not allow a convincing assessment to be made by scientific means as to whether and, if so, in what way the central bank councils will change the money supply in the coming years. In principle, we do not know how the market participants will react to the factors influencing them in the future—economic upswings or downturns, technical innovations, natural phenomena, or political events—and we do not know today with certainty the conditions and circumstances under which action will be taken.

What can be said with certainty, however, is that all statements that can be derived without contradiction from the logic of human action can claim strict generality and that they necessarily always and without exception apply, today and tomorrow. Doubts about this statement can be refuted: "It does not matter for man whether or not beyond the sphere accessible to the human mind there are other spheres in which there is something categorically different from human thinking and acting. No knowledge from such spheres penetrates to the human mind."[70] There is only *one* logic of action that is conceivable for humans and that can be understood by the human mind.

With the help of the logic of human action, however, it can already be said today that the decision of the central bank councils to increase the money supply necessarily leads to a reduction in the purchasing power of money—compared to a situation in which the money supply has not been increased. If the money supply in the hands of the market participants increases, the marginal utility of the additionally received monetary unit decreases in comparison to the other goods. As a result, the market participants exchange the new money for goods, provided that the demand for money remains unchanged. The result is an increase in the price of goods, which reduces the purchasing power of money. (This, by the way, is the reason why the "classical economists" called the expansion of the money supply "inflation": for them, the increase in the money supply was the *cause* of the price increases; they saw the *effect* of the increased money supply in the rising prices.)

[70] Mises, *Human Action*, p. 36.

However, the price effect that can ultimately be observed depends on the particular circumstances. It is conceivable that the increase in the money supply will increase the prices of goods and reduce the purchasing power of money. It is also possible, however, that goods prices will remain unchanged—for example, because a *positive supply shock* occurred at the same time, which had a price-reducing effect. If this overlays the price-increasing effect of the money supply expansion and the prices of goods therefore remain unchanged, the statement of the a priori theory nevertheless applies, namely, that an increase in the money supply reduces the purchasing power of money (compared to a situation in which the money supply has not been expanded).

The a priori theory can also be applied to the assessment of the economic and social consequences of the existence of the state or the coexistence of many states. Such conceptual progress (*progression*) amounts to a conditional impact assessment on the basis of a priori science of action. It can claim—as long as the conditions under which the action takes place are realistic—to provide a conditional, rational, and realistic assessment of the future.

Such a train of thought was developed in chapter eight. In retrospect, the *a priori* theory identified the steps by which the state gradually acquired sovereignty over money production and replaced the initially available commodity or gold money with its own fiat money. The following chapter, the first chapter of the second part of this book, is about extending action-logical thinking to the future. It will explore where the coexistence in today's world of many states, which more or less all adhere to democratic socialism, leads. The result of these considerations is revealed in the next chapter title: "The Progression Theorem: Toward World Government."

PART TWO

CHAPTER 12

THE PROGRESSION THEOREM: TOWARD A WORLD GOVERNMENT

All nations must come together to build a stronger global regime.
– **BARACK OBAMA**

The idea of establishing *world domination, a world government, a world state* is not new—and it results from experience with the aggressive, warlike nature of the state. Immanuel Kant in his late work "Zum ewigen Frieden" ("Perpetual Peace") (1795) promoted a *world republic* in order to achieve a lasting peace between the states; in doing so he took up the ideas of the Dutch legal scholar Hugo Grotius (1583–1645). The English writer H. G. Wells (1866–1946) strongly promoted the idea of a world state in various books. The English historian Arnold J. Toynbee (1889–1975) and the American historian and philosopher Will J. Durant (1885–1981) were also in favor.

The League of Nations since 1920 and the United Nations since 1945 are modern attempts to approach the "ideal of world government"—not only to promote international cooperation and peacefully balance the interests of the various states, but also to fundamentally support the interests of the state.[71] The G20 (Group of Twenty), an informal association of nineteen states and the European Union, is an initiative by these states to shape the international financial and economic system and to coordinate policies that, it is thought, can only be pursued jointly at the international level—such as environmental protection, migration management, and counterterrorism.

[71] Leopold Kohr writes bluntly: "The League of Nations was the product of World War I, and the United Nations of World War II. None of these glorified vast-scale organizations was ever worth its price, and it makes one shudder to think of the price of an ultimate single World State." (Kohr, *The Breakdown of Nations* [Devon, UK: Green Books, 2001], p. 74.)

In 1961, the British philosopher Bertrand Russell (1872-1970) published a paper entitled "Has Man a Future?" in which he argued that the whole world needed a single government to maintain peace; as early as 1955, Russell had published the "Russell Einstein Manifesto" with Albert Einstein (1879-1955), in which he sought to warn of the dangers of nuclear war.

The idea of a world state continues to receive support from many sides. With a view to a possible clash of cultures, the Catholic theologian Hans Küng (b. 1928), together with representatives of various religions, adopted Towards a Global Ethic: An Initial Declaration in 1993: a commitment to nonviolence, reverence for life, a just economic order, a life in truth, and equal rights for men and women. Without a *global ethic* there could be no world order. The philosopher Otfried Höffe (b. 1943) also formulates a need for action in *Demokratie im Zeitalter der Globalisierung* (1999), in which he argues that in order to meet future challenges, there is a need for a global legal and state order which has to submit to the conditions of a liberal democracy and which is supplemented in a subsidiary way by the national states.

The numerous explanations and design recommendations for the international coexistence of states, however, usually ignore logical findings.[72] This deficit will be remedied below.

At the beginning of 2019, there were 195 states in the world.[73] Such a large number of states does not, however, represent an end stage or a stable equilibrium from a logical point of view. Rather, the multitude of states existing side by side has a powerful tendency—namely the tendency to make fewer and fewer states out of many states and ultimately to form a unified world state. Hans-Hermann Hoppe takes this position in his 1990 essay "Banking, Nation States, and International Politics: A Sociological Reconstruction of the Present Economic Order,"[74] in which

---

[72] For example Herfried Münkler explicitly addresses "the logic of world domination" (the subtitle of his book) and bases his argument on "the rationality of the actors, simply the logic of world domination" (*Imperien: Die Logik der Weltherrschaft—vom alten Rom bis zu den Vereinigten Staaten* [Berlin: Rowohlt, 2005], p. 9). However, the logical insight that the state has an aggressive urge to expand (in a way that violates property ownership) is ignored.

[73] One hundred and ninety-three states are members of the United Nations, and two are not (Vatican City and Palestine); not included are Taiwan, the Cook Islands, Niue, dependencies and others.

[74] This is a counterposition to the widespread view that a balance between a few large states would be established in the world. For example, George Bernard Shaw (1856-1950), member of the socialist intellectual Fabian Society, argued, "The world is to the big and powerful states by necessity: and the little ones must come within their borders or be crushed out of existence," quoting Elie Halevy, *A History of the English People*, epilogue vol. I, 1895-1905, trans. E. I. Watkin (London: Ernest Benn, 1929), p. 105n1.

he formulates a *progression-theoretical reflection*.[75]

A state—understood as a territorial *compulsory monopolist with ultimate decision-making power over all conflicts in its territory*—is necessarily in competition with other states. In principle, every state must fear that its subjects will leave if it gives them too raw a deal. For example, companies relocate their operations to other countries if they are overtaxed in their home country. Moreover, the possibility of any state to finance itself by spending inflationary money is limited. If inflation rises too much, people will no longer accept state money and will, for example, ask for comparatively better money from other countries.

How can the state overcome the limitations that stand in the way of its own urge to exploit and expand? The states could think about cartel formation. However, a cartel, in so far as it is based on voluntary agreement, is unstable. The cartel members would be obliged to imitate the economic and tax policy of the worst cartel member, so that no location has better economic conditions than the least attractive—otherwise there would be a migration of capital and labor between regions, which the cartel is meant to prevent. However, the comparatively better states will not want to get involved in such a policy. For them the incentives to withdraw from the cartel are greatest: they can offer better economic and living conditions within their borders and thus attract companies and workers from other countries, thereby broadening their own tax and power base.

Couldn't a state cartel try to prevent an unwelcome withdrawal of cartel members by contractually agreeing that in such a case painful sanctions would become due, for example, in the form of capital movement restrictions and trade sanctions? At least that's conceivable. But who would want to voluntarily sign such a contract? Certainly not the states that operate better than the others, i.e., those that have the greatest incentive to leave the cartel because cartel membership does not benefit them.

Because a cartel of states is not stable, Hoppe argues, there is only one stable solution: a state must eliminate the competitive situation, expand its sphere of influence and, as its ultimate goal, establish itself as

---

[75] Briefly stated, the term progression theorem, which was coined by Joseph T. Salerno, "Two Traditions in Modern Monetary Theory: John Law and A. R. J. Turgot," in *Money: Sound and Unsound* (Auburn, AL: Ludwig von Mises Institute, 2010), pp. 1–60, esp. 49), refers to a *path-dependent advance in action-logical thinking*: What logical consequences result when action is taken under certain conditions created by the preceding action? For an application of this thereom, see Jörg Guido Hülsmann, "Political Unification: A Generalized Progression Theorem," *Journal of Libertarian Studies* 13, no. 1 (1997): 81–96.

a world government and then turn its money into world money. It's obvious who wins in this battle: it will be the economically and militarily most powerful state. It can quite easily expand its sphere of influence by violent measures (war): it invades other states and subdues and dominates them; its threat potential alone may be sufficient for other states to comply with it and to submit to it voluntarily.

The most powerful state also ensures that the defeated states accept its currency—its fiat money. The advantages this has for it are obvious: the more people use its money, the greater the money-creation gain (seigniorage). What's more, once the most powerful state has a monopoly over the production of the money used worldwide, its financing possibilities and thus its taxation and redistribution power increase enormously. It is easier than ever to buy support from its electorate—the cost of fiat funding is borne not only by local citizens and entrepreneurs, but also by the people in the subdued countries.

However, an alternative, pseudo-peaceful development to the militant and violent rise of a state to a world state is conceivable: democratic socialism *becomes the dominant, universally accepted ideology worldwide*, and from then on it determines the form of relations between states. When the states have established democratic socialism, there will also be agreement that democratic socialism strives for world domination. The democratic socialists cannot be content with just creating equality for the people in a region. This does not achieve equality for all people in all regions of the world at the same time.

In addition to equality, there is another very practical reason why democratic socialism must claim worldwide applicability: a spatially limited democratic socialism cannot exist permanently in the face of a free market system. Efficient enterprises and employees will emigrate from a spatially limited democratic socialism. In view of the "better conditions" in the other regions, sooner or later the electorate will demand a departure from democratic socialism, or the poor economic and social conditions will force this.

But even a coexistence of regionally or nationally different forms of democratic socialism cannot function in the long run. They too would compete for capital and labor. As long as economic conditions vary from region to region (due to differences in resources and population density), there will be incentives for workers to migrate and for companies to relocate capital between them. The individual states that have committed themselves to democratic socialism will not be able to put up with this.[76]

Democratic socialism will have to aspire to world domination under a unified leadership.[77] However, it will find itself confronted with great difficulties. One reason is the diversity of production conditions in this world. There are regions that have better and richer stocks of natural resources than others—and as a result, prosperity can vary from region to region. Another reason is that the population also varies from region to region: there are relatively dense and less densely populated areas. Regions with a relatively large labor supply will have lower real incomes than regions with a relatively low labor supply.

In order to bring about equal living conditions, the democratic socialists must allow migration or initiate and control it politically. People must move from regions with less favorable production conditions to regions with more favorable production conditions. If migration were possible without hindrance, sooner or later a situation would arise in which wages for equal work would converge worldwide. Some areas would be denser, others less densely populated: In net-emigration countries, the labor supply would shrink, and real wages rise; in net-immigration countries, labor supply would rise and real wages fall.

In the world today we find, however, that unimpeded migration inevitably leads to a problem for democratic socialism. Due to the diversity of people in this world (in terms of language, culture, tradition, religion, etc.), democratic socialism is not faced with a homogeneous population, but rather with a highly heterogeneous electorate in the individual regions of the world. This makes a politically motivated redistribution of income and wealth between heterogeneous voters difficult or even impossible: people in different regions will take the view that the resources and capital in their territory must serve them and that outsiders must not benefit from them.

It is certainly possible to implement democratic socialism in individual regions in which people feel relatively closely connected on the basis of language, culture, tradition, religion, etc. Here there is probably at least a certain willingness on the part of those who have some of their

[76] In democratic socialism—as in every democracy—the struggle for prerogatives is unleashed: each tries to forestall the other, to gain more privileges than the others. There will always be winners and losers—simply because there cannot be privileges for everyone!

[77] We can also say *centralistic socialism*. See Michael Tugan-Baranowsky, *Der moderne Sozialismus in seiner geschichtlichen Entwicklung* (Dresden: O. V. Böhmert, 1908), p. 132.

wealth taken away to agree to the redistribution or to accept it without insurrection. If, however, the composition of the population is too heterogeneous, democratic socialism loses its support among voters. This points to the central obstacle that stands in the way of the goal of establishing a worldwide uniform democratic socialism: the diversity of people. This insight draws attention to the *nation* and the *nationality principle.*

CHAPTER 13

THE NATION: COMMUNITY OF LANGUAGE AND VALUES

There is no such thing as chance;
and what seem to us merest
accident springs from the
deepest source of destiny.[78]
– **FRIEDRICH SCHILLER**

With the help of the logic of human action we can explain the origin and meaning of *nation and the nationality principle.*

Looking back far into the history of humankind, it can be seen that people first came together in small units (first in nomadic clans, later, when they settled down, in village communities), because they recognized that the *division of labor* was useful. The division of labor and the trade in goods produced by the division of labor are particularly supported by the development of a common language. A small unit organized according to the division of labor therefore becomes a language community (and usually also a community of rules and values). This is the birth of the nation.

The core of a nation is a linguistic community. The origin of the nation can be traced back, by means of logical considerations of action, to the human insight into the higher productivity of acting together and working together through the division of labor. In that sense, the nation is indeed something natural. In Europe, the nation appeared as a political phenomenon when, in the eighteenth and nineteenth centuries, people began to rebel against foreign rule—to which they were exposed from within as well as from without—and to assert their *right to self-determination.*[79] The nation

[78] Friedrich Schiller, *Wallensteins, Tod* (Berlin: Aufbau Taschenbuch Verlag, 1999), p. 381.
[79] The foreign domination to which an individual is exposed exists externally and internally. Then as now, internal foreign rule is usually less obvious than the external.

as a political phenomenon has its roots in the struggle for its own freedom. The formation of the nation is not per se associated with hostility between different nations.

THE NATION AS A LANGUAGE COMMUNITY

Is it convenient to link a common language with the core of the nation? First of all, the enormous importance of language for thinking, for the exchange of ideas, for togetherness in daily life speaks in favor of this. Thinking cannot be communicated other than linguistically. And language is not a private matter. The philosopher Ludwig Wittgenstein (1889–1951) has shown that there can be no such thing as a *private language* (which only I understand and which I cannot share with anyone). Language guarantees the possibility of intersubjectivity; it presupposes a communication community—speaking with others.

Perhaps there is still reluctance to see the essence of the nation in the linguistic community? This may be mainly due to some apparent demarcation difficulties, which, however, can be resolved. Nation and language are not unchangeable categories; they can change over time.

The mastery of language determines the degree of belonging to a nation. The educated are fully a part of the nation, the less educated only as far as the understanding of language is accessible to them.

Most people belong to only one nation. But there are also people who have mastered several languages and can think in, and speak, them almost perfectly. They then belong to several nations or language communities.

The nation *does not* entail the need for different parts of the nation to converge to form a unitary state. From this point of view, for example, English and Americans—who both use the English language—can be seen as one nation.

This also applies to Danes and Norwegians. After the separation of Norway from Denmark in 1814, an attempt was made to revive the Norwegian language. Since this is strongly based on Danish, this was mainly done by enriching Danish with some expressions from Norwegian dialects. Although today they form two politically separate states, Danes and Norwegians belong to one language-nation.

In Ireland, almost all inhabitants now speak English. Gaelic, which was still dominant in Ireland at the beginning of the nineteenth century, was afterward strongly suppressed for various reasons and, despite strong promotion after Ireland's independence, could no longer regain its former status. The differences between the Republic of Ireland and the United Kingdom's Northern Ireland are social and religious, not national.

Different nations will enter into a peaceful and productive division of labor with each other when the conditions for this division of labor are in place. This observation comes from the British economist David Ricardo. He showed that it makes sense for people in the respective nations to concentrate on producing the goods in which production they have cost advantages. And that it makes sense to enter into the division of labor even when people in one nation can produce *all* goods at the lowest cost. It is advantageous for the nation which is superior in all areas of production to turn to the production of goods for which its superiority is greater, and to leave the production of other goods, for which it is also, but to a lesser extent, superior, to the less favored nation.

The problem of aggressive rivalry between nations only arose when the state—understood as the territorial monopolist of the final decisions on all conflicts in its territory—seized the nation by roping it in for its own purposes. The buzzword at this point is the *nationality principle*: Every nation should have its own state. While the nation, as already mentioned, has a natural origin, the nationality principle is a purely artificial product. The nationality principle is not natural, it cannot be justified logically, it is rather a phenomenon that stems from political and ideological considerations.

The nation is an obstacle to the attempt to place different nations under a central authority, a unitary state. Even the German philosopher and poet Johann Gottfried Herder (1744–1803) knew about the unreasonableness of wanting to place national character traits under a unified state leadership. He wrote: "A people/nation [*Volk*] is both a plant of nature and a family; only one with several branches. Nothing, then, seems so obviously contrary to the purpose of governments as the unnatural enlargement of states, the wild mixing of human ethnicities under one scepter."[80]

The proponents of democratic socialism, therefore, want to bear down on the nation and the nationality principle. They wish to abolish national sovereignty and shift it to supranational levels. For example, for decades, the aspirations of the "political globalists" in Europe have aimed to remove the nationality principle from the world, in order—ultimately—to create a "United States of Europe": a construct in which the rights of national parliamentary self-determination are abolished and replaced by a central government power.

The effort to relativize the nationality principle or to abolish it in the long term is also evident at the global level, in the political efforts to increasingly coordinate national policy fields—such as monetary and fiscal policy. These include, for example, the G20, which since 1999 has represented nineteen independent states and the states of the European Union—and thus the most important industrialized and emerging countries in the world. The G20 is not a world government, but in the longer term its political thrust is tantamount to the desire to establish a world government, a world state.

The bond between the nationality principle and the nation is much less close than it may seem at first glance: the nationality principle needs the nation, but the nation does not need the nationality principle. While it is politically possible to eliminate the nationality principle—especially since this is only a politically arbitrary institution—this does not apply equally to the nation—whose existence has an action-logical foundation.

Is it conceivable that the nation—understood as a self-contained language community—would dissolve, that at some point the multitude of nations existing in this world today would form themselves into a single nation, in the course of a voluntary decision by the people? Under what conditions would that be possible? One force of change that needs

[80] Johann Gottfried Herder, *Ideen zur Philosophie der Geschichte der Menschheit* (Karlsruhe, Germany, 1794), p. 315. With regard to Europe, the French writer Michel Houellebecq (b. 1958) expressed himself entirely in line with Herder's thoughts: "It is my conviction that we in Europe have neither a common language nor common values nor common interests, that, in one word, Europe does not exist and that it will never form a people/nation or support a possible democracy, simply because it does not want to form a people/nation. Europe is just a stupid idea that has turned into a bad dream from which we should perhaps wake up." Quoted in Hannah Lühmann, "Europa, eine dämliche Idee," *Die Welt*, Dec. 14, 2017, www.welt.de/kultur/literarischewelt/plus185548620/Michel-Houellebecq-Europaeine-daemliche-Idee.html.

to be considered in this context is the long-term impact of the international division of labor.

It has already been mentioned that David Ricardo explained the division of labor between people from different nations through the *theory of relative cost advantages*. However, Ricardo's theory is based on a very important assumption: labor and capital are internationally immobile. But what if capital is mobile and labor immobile? In this case, capital moves to the regions of the world where it can achieve the highest yield.

It is removed from regions where it is relatively abundant and generates relatively low returns and shifted to regions where it is relatively scarce and can generate relatively high returns. The redistribution of capital leads to a global alignment of the marginal efficiency of capital. Because the labor factor is immobile, there will continue to be areas that are relatively densely populated and areas that are less densely populated. Consequently, there will be no equalization of wages for equal work in the world: wages will tend to remain lower in densely populated areas and higher in less densely populated areas.

This scenario does not lead to an equalization of wages for equal work in the world, but it does lead to a more efficient allocation of capital and thus to a welfare gain. Although it is conceivable that the intensity of the division of labor and trade will also increase, it is assumed that there will be no immigration or emigration in the respective national territories. In this scenario there is no need and no incentive for people in the respective nations to turn away from their national affiliation and identity. In other words: in a world where capital is mobile but labor immobile, people tend to remain loyal to their nation, not to turn away from it. But what if capital *and* labor were mobile?

If not, only capital migrates to the regions of the world where it achieves the highest returns, but if labor can also move unchecked to where it achieves the highest wages, the question arises: Would the disappearance, the dissolution of the nation take place under the condition of international capital mobility and unchecked migration? Would, sooner or later, something like a worldwide united nation emerge, playing into the hands of democratic socialism? The following chapter provides an answer to this important question.

CHAPTER 14

MIGRATION: NATURAL AND UNNATURAL

Due to the interdependence of thought and word it is clear that languages are not really a means to represent the truth that is already known, but rather a means to discover the previously unrecognized truth. What makes them different is not their sounds and signs, but their world views.[81]

– **ALEXANDER VON HUMBOLDT**

The diversity of living conditions in this world has always triggered migrations of individuals and entire peoples throughout history. There will also be reasons for migration in the future. For example, new technologies can make locations that were previously unattractive attractive, and vice versa. The same can happen because of climatic changes. Economically, it can be said that when capital and labor are internationally mobile, the absolute costs will decide where capital will be invested in the world and where people will want to settle.

Job seekers migrate from regions where marginal labor productivity and hence wages are low to regions where marginal productivity and hence wages are higher. This reduces the supply of labor in the areas from which people emigrate—and increases the marginal productivity of labor and thereby wages. On the other hand, labor supply increases in the immigration areas and marginal labor productivity and wages decline here as a result of the now increased labor supply.

[81] Wilhelm von Humboldt, *Über das vergleichende Sprachstudium in Beziehung auf die verschiedenen Epochen der Sprachentwicklung* (Berlin, 1820), p. 255.

With free mobility of labor, migration continues until the same marginal productivity for the same work prevails everywhere in the world. Different regions of the world will then have differences in their population density, but equal wages for equal work will be paid worldwide. In this way, the productivity of the work is optimally exploited. That is the economic law of *migration*. If we want to apply it to the present situation, we must bear in mind that a world has arisen in which land is no longer a free good but is privately or publicly owned. The significance of this "restriction" for migration becomes clear when we consider migration under two conditions: (1) migration in a free economy and society without a state and (2) migration in an unfree economy and society with a state.

Considering (1) in a liberal economy and society, unconditional respect for property applies—understood as self-ownership of one's own body and of the goods legally acquired in a nonaggressive way. If property is accepted in this way, the migration of persons between regions is possible, but only if the owners of land expressly issue an invitation.

Every property owner has the right to invite guests into his house and onto his land. He or his guest must pay for the costs of travel, accommodation, meals, and clothing. Companies are allowed to hire employees as they wish. However, employees will only (be able to) accept the job offer if the companies pay wages with which the employees can finance their way of life.

Uninvited immigration—entering an area of land owned by a person or community who has not invited them to enter—is tantamount to infringing property rights, and the owners will justifiably defend themselves against it. In a free economy and society (without the state) there would be no systematic migration problem in the sense of unwanted movements of people. There may be some cases of uninvited visitors here and there, but no chronic uninvited migration.

Considering (2) if a state exists and its immigration policy violates the property rights of the people in the country of immigration, the picture changes. As is well known, the state opens up the possibility for some to assert their special interests and privileges. This inevitably leads to strife that ignites due to conflicting interests. For example, workers whose wages are falling as a result of immigration will call on their unions to demand immigration restrictions: the wages of domestic workers decrease when the domestic labor supply increases.

However, immigration restrictions put domestic entrepreneurs at a disadvantage: they have to pay higher wages and make correspondingly lower profits compared to a situation in which there are no immigration restrictions. Domestic production is lower and more expensive than it could be with immigration. Businesses will therefore also seek to use their influence in policymaking to facilitate immigration.

Political programs will also want to influence immigration policy. A motive can be the humane desire to alleviate need: people from countries with low incomes should be allowed to immigrate in order to lead a better life. Or the motive may be to avert the economic consequences of a shrinking population through immigration. Another motive springs from the idea that world peace is promoted when people of different descent, different cultural and religious backgrounds do not live far apart from one another but in close proximity.

The objective of the democratic socialists in this dispute is to abolish the principle of the nation-state and above all to abolish the nation. This is an indispensable, a necessary condition for opening up the possibility of creating a unitary nation and a unitary state in the first place. But how can that succeed? For example, how about the following idea: the nations will be unified by eliminating through migration the spatial separation that has existed so far between regions with national populations?

This could happen, for example, by forced resettlement. However, at present it is very unlikely that political majorities in support of this can be found in the nation-state democracies. The costs and suffering that forced resettlement would entail for the people affected—the displaced persons as well as the "hosts"—would be too great. An alternative route to this is politically controlled migration: the nation-states are opened up to immigration from outside; above all immigration is promoted for those whose language and culture are foreign. But could the nations really be dissolved in this way?

If immigrants assimilate linguistically and culturally—if they abandon the language, customs, and religion of their country of origin and adopt those of the country of immigration—the nation-states remain homogeneous in themselves but at the same time heterogeneous among themselves. This applies both to the nation into which immigration is taking place and whose population is increasing, and to the nation from which emigration is taking place and which is decreasing in number. If, on the other hand, immigrants fail to assimilate, the country of immigration becomes heterogeneous: it will become a region in which other nations will establish themselves alongside the nation that has been the state-defining nation up to that point.

The supporters of a unified international democratic socialism must therefore rely on immigration *not* leading to assimilation.[82] Admittedly, unassimilated immigration does not guarantee the dissolution of the nation and the nation-state principle. But it at least opens up the possibility that, at least in the country of immigration, the nation and the nation-state principle will be pushed back and perhaps ultimately dissolved. In this context, however, the following is particularly serious: immigration leads to a particularly thorny problem in a country of immigration where the democratic majority principle prevails.[83]

The greater the role of the state in economic and social life, the more bitter the political struggle for the majority position will be, and the greater the *political powerlessness* of those who lose out in this struggle, those who end up in the minority position. Tensions between the people who are in the majority and the people who represent the minority are inevitable in a democracy, in democratic socialism. However, they are mitigated in areas where the population is relatively closely linked by language, customs, tradition, culture, and religion.[84] The majority here will not completely lose sight of the interests of the minority; and the minority will also be prepared to bow to the majority to some extent, albeit grudgingly.

The picture changes dramatically when people with very different linguistic and cultural backgrounds live together in the same area. The majority principle then ensures that the minority here is immediately oppressed. The majority has little or no incentive to give any special consideration to a minority that seems fundamentally alien to them. The minority therefore has only two alternatives: either it assimilates, or it does not assimilate.

The case of voluntary assimilation is associated with the least problems. The immigrants gradually adopt the language and habits of the

---

[82] As a rule of thumb, the greater the number of immigrants per year compared to the population in the host country, the greater the likelihood that immigrants will not assimilate.

[83] This is pointed out by Ludwig von Mises, *Nation, Staat und Wirtschaft: Beiträge zur Politik und Geschichte der Zeit* (Vienna: Manz'sche Verlags- und Universitäts-Buchhandlung, 1919), pp. 31–45.

[84] This notion can be found, e.g., in F. A. Hayek, *The Road to Serfdom* (London: Routledge Classics, 2001), p. 144: "The belief in the community of aims and interests with fellow-men seems to presuppose a greater degree of similarity of outlook and thought than exists between men merely as human beings."

people in the country of immigration and become part of the nation of the country of immigration. If the immigrants do not wish to assimilate, they remain a minority and are excluded from political decision-making. They lose their self-determination. Either they come to terms with it or they may want to protest—for example, by trying to become the majority in the country of immigration.

In the case, however, where non-assimilated immigrants seek the majority position (e.g., through further immigration or high birth rates), the inhabitants of the country to which they immigrate have to fear that they will fall behind. Either they submit to the fate of being ousted from their previous majority position in the future or they oppose the fact that immigrants ascend to the majority—for example by forcing assimilation. There will be conflict when the inhabitants of the immigration country force immigrants to assimilate but the immigrants preserve their peculiarities and do not want to give them up.

We recognize that democracy (if understood as the right to self-determination) proves to be not a peacemaker in a linguistically and culturally heterogeneous population, but a cause or aggravator of conflict. For supporters of international democratic socialism, this means that attempting to heterogenize or abolish the nation-state through politically controlled migration is not a viable way to maintain democracy.

Rather, democratic socialism must abandon its democratic roots and transform itself into a totalitarian socialism if it is to ascend to a unified global system. However, in public the democratic socialists never tire of expressing their inseparability with democracy. What to make of that? Not too much: the democratic solidarity of democratic socialism turns out to be a bogus claim, according to the "iron law of the oligarchy." This "law" states that party democracy forms an oligarchized elite rule that silently and secretly undermines and controls democracy. The significance of this for the possibility of establishing a world state with a world currency is discussed in the following chapter.

CHAPTER 15

THE ILLUSION OF DEMOCRACY: THE "IRON LAW OF OLIGARCHY"

The danger is obvious that the social revolution would change the tangible and visible ruling class of today, openly recognized as such, into a secret demagogic oligarchy operating under the guise of equality.
— **ROBERT MICHELS**

In 1911, the German-Italian sociologist Robert Michels (1876–1936) published his book *Zur Soziologie des Parteiwesens in der modernen Demokratie: Untersuchungen über die oligarchischen Tendenzen des Gruppenlebens (Political Parties: A Sociological Study of the Oligarchical Tendencies of Modern Democracy).* In it, he formulates the "iron law of the oligarchy." In democracies, according to Michels, there is a tendency toward oligarchy: the rule of the few over the many.[85] Sooner or later, a small group, the cunning, power-hungry party elites, will rule. There emerges a reign of the elected over the voters. It is therefore an illusion to believe that democracy gives voters self-determination over their destinies. Michels suggests three reasons that explain the shift of power from the voters, from the party base, to the elected.

First, self-government of the masses is not possible, not even technically. Democracy needs parties. Parties are organizations, and like any

[85] In addition to Michels, Vilfredo Pareto (1848–1923), Gaetano Mosca (1858–1941) and José Ortega y Gasset (1883–1955) are among the most important thinkers who have dealt with elite rule. The British historian Niall Ferguson (b. 1964) has recently subjected the topic to a new perspective in his book *The Square and the Tower: Networks, Hierarchies and the Struggle for Global Power* (London: Penguin Random House UK, 2017) as competition between hierarchies and networks.

organization, a party needs firm leadership. This puts people in positions who have the necessary aptitude (expertise, leadership, assertiveness, etc.). A professional leadership emerges. Second, the mass of voters is ignorant and not the sovereign masters of their own destinies. The majority of people are not in a position to form their political will in a rational manner. They're looking for political leadership. Third, the members of the party elites have the personal, intellectual, and also charismatic superiority to win over the masses and the party delegates and to create a following for themselves.

Once the relatively small group of party elites has reached the power centers–once a *party oligarchy* has developed–it begins, according to Michels, to isolate and shield itself from competitors. Because of their intellectual superiority, their will to assert themselves and their access to financial resources, the members of the elite can secure their fame as public elected representatives, make their actions appear to be directed toward the welfare of society, make themselves personally inviolable, and silence political counter currents.[86] The party oligarchs use their incontestable position of power for their own purposes. They begin to pursue goals that are no longer consistent with the party base or the will of the voters.

Can Michel's theses be transferred to the present? Does it offer a suitable pattern of interpretation for today's sociopolitical events? One might first think that the "oligarchization of democracy" is kept in check if there is effective competition between parties for government power. As long as voters can give their votes to competing parties, oligarchization within the individual party may occur, but not oligarchization of government power per se. But this hope proves to be deceptive.

All parties are wooing for votes. And the voters give their vote to the parties whose programs and policies they hope will improve their personal position. The parties therefore have an incentive not only to attend upon voters' dreams of redistribution but also to encourage them. In the competition for government power, those who want to be elected to power outbid each other in winning as many voters as possible with "election gifts." It is precisely this buying of votes, which takes place in democracy, that supports Michels's thesis.

---

[86] F. A. Hayek dealt with the question in detail as early as 1944: Why do the worst reach the top in socialist apparatuses? See Hayek, *The Road to Serfdom*, chap. 10.

Every form of rule—whether dictatorship, aristocracy, or democracy—depends on approval, at least on tolerance by public opinion. The rulers are outnumbered by the ruled. Should the conviction spread among the governed that they must get rid of the rulers, an overthrow would be inevitable. The parties and the party oligarchs know that. In order to maintain their power, they therefore rely on "persuasion," for example, by ensuring that in education and training, people are taught the indispensability of the democratic party system. In addition, they follow a *divide et impera principle*: divide and rule. Tax revenues are used to pay for votes. And to avoid any resistance, everything is done to dispel the suspicion that there are "net tax victims" and "net tax profiteers."

However, because all parties compete in the same way for the favor of the majority, the content of their programs more or less converges. In fact, a party cartel emerges that paves the way for the oligarchization of democracy. And once party competition has been paralyzed, the party oligarchs have a wide scope of action. Extreme policies can then be implemented relatively easily, which would not be so easily possible if grassroots democracy were operating—such as the dismantling of national sovereignty in favor of supranational authorities or the "policy of open borders."

"Political globalism"—the endeavor not to leave the economic and social coexistence of people on this planet to the free market but to steer it according to political goals—bears the unmistakable signature of an oligarchized democratic socialism: small groups make far-reaching decisions, often in back rooms; special interests (of banks and large corporations) gain privileges; parliamentarians willingly give a leg up to the oligarchized rule. If one follows Michels, there is no reason to believe that in democracy (more precisely, in democratic socialism) the will of the voters determines the government. Rather, the power goes to the oligarchized elite rulership.

There is another aspect that needs to be addressed here: the role of professionals in the institutions that democratic socialism generates in large numbers. These institutions—whether social security, pension or health insurance, central banks or financial supervisory authorities—have one thing in common: they are characterized by growing complexity and confusion. The reason: all these state institutions are developed, managed, and changed by so-called experts, experts in their field. Outsiders can't contribute anything.

And so, it is the experts who are asked by politicians for their opinion when something does not work, and solutions are sought. However, the experts are not only distinguished by the fact that they are experts in their field. They stand out above all because they unreservedly support the principles on which the institutions are built. When problems arise, they will therefore adapt and change the institutions, but always respecting the principles on which they are built: "Once the apparatus is established, its future development will be shaped by what those who have chosen to serve it regard as its needs."[87]

It is the experts in particular who create *path dependency*: Once they are made, decisions limit the scope of future decision-making; revision or abandoning the path taken becomes increasingly difficult. How can democratic socialism and its oligarchic leadership take advantage of this path dependency? As shown in the previous chapter, the attempt to build a worldwide democratic socialism by unifying in terms of language, culture, and religion the populations of the different nations of the world through migration would face great, seemingly insurmountable obstacles.

Another, more promising possibility for democratic socialists is to create a single world currency. That would have two advantages. After all, having *one* currency for the world is economically optimal—this was shown in chapter 8. On the other hand, the current system of national state fiat monies can be simply, at least from a technical point of view, converted into one *fiat* world currency and steered by one world central bank—and thus the worldwide economic and social development would *be subject* to a central political leadership to an extent previously unknown.

For the proponents of democratic socialism, the creation of a unified world currency is therefore an extremely attractive strategy for putting into practice their constructivist dream of steering the social and economic events on this planet according to their political demands. If we look at recent monetary history since the end of the Second World War, we can clearly see how far the ideas of democratic socialism have already influenced the world monetary system. This will be examined in more detail in the following chapter.

---

[87] F. A. Hayek, *The Constitution of Liberty* (Chicago: University of Chicago Press, 1960), p. 291.

CHAPTER 16

DOLLAR IMPERIALISM: THE BRETTON WOODS SYSTEM

One of the factors that contributes to the great confidence in the United States dollar which exists the world over ... is undoubtedly our large gold holdings. ...

[I]nternational agreement is not a substitute for gold.

– **HARRY DEXTER WHITE**

With the beginning of the First World War the era of the worldwide gold money ends. Unbacked paper money (or: fiat money) becomes standard money. But this type of money causes many problems: it causes inflation and exchange rate fluctuations that affect the global division of labor and trade. The international community of states therefore tries to continue the tradition of using gold money. But it will only be a half-hearted and therefore misguided attempt. From July 1 to July 22, 1944, the finance ministers and central bank governors of forty-four states of the later victorious powers met in Bretton Woods, New Hampshire. The aim of this international monetary and financial conference is to work out how to reorganize the world financial system for the period after the end of the Second World War.[88] The British supported the *Keynes Plan* (named after John Maynard Keynes, 1883–1946), the Americans the *White Plan* (named after Harry D. White, 1892–1948).[89]

---

[88] A good overview is provided by the Federal Reserve Bank of Boston, *The International Monetary System: Forty Years after Bretton Woods, Proceedings of a Conference Held at Bretton Woods, New Hampshire* (Boston: Federal Reserve Bank of Boston, 1984).

[89] For details see International Monetary Fund, *The International Monetary Fund, 1945–1965: Twenty Years of International Monetary Cooperation*, vol. 3, *Documents*, ed. J. Keith Horsefield (Washington, DC: International Monetary Fund, 1969), pp. 3–96.

The result of the conference is the *Bretton Woods system*. It is marked by three characteristics. *First*, the new monetary system is designed as a *gold exchange standard*. Gold is the only internationally recognized means of payment in 1944 and is used to settle cross-border trade. The gold-backed US dollar is elevated to become the world's reserve currency, as from 1934, thirty-five US dollars were worth one troy ounce of gold. The US Federal Reserve promises to redeem US dollar holdings held by other central banks into physical gold at any time and without restriction. This promise of the Americans is believed, because at the time the monetary agreement is signed, they have about three-quarters of the world's currency gold at their disposal, and because hardly anyone can imagine that the United States would one day have chronic balance-of-payments deficits (i.e., permanently import more than export and thus suffer from a gold outflow).

Second, the Bretton Woods system provides for fixed exchange rates. All participating currencies have a fixed exchange ratio (parity) against the US dollar. In this way they are indirectly tied to gold. The currency of a participating country may only fluctuate around parity within a narrow range of a maximum of ± 1 percent. If, for example, the deutschmark is under revaluation pressure against the US dollar, the Deutsche Bundesbank is obliged to intervene in the foreign exchange market: it has to buy US dollars and put them into circulation until the exchange rate is back within the specified exchange rate range. There is no obligation for the US Federal Reserve to intervene.

Third, in the Bretton Woods system, currencies are freely interchangeable (convertible) between themselves. For example, on the foreign exchange markets, German marks, British pounds, and French francs can be exchanged for US dollars. The US dollars can be exchanged for physical gold at the US Federal Reserve on request. However, this exchange possibility only exists for payments between central banks. Moreover, currency convertibility is initially limited to payment transactions for commodities. It does not exist for the autonomous movement of capital. It was not until 1958 that convertibility was introduced for capital movements independent of trade in goods.

The Bretton Woods system basically does not deserve to be described as a form of gold standard—although that is often the case today. Rather, it was a "pseudo-gold standard." But at least the Bretton Woods system initially contributes to reviving world trade in the immediate postwar period and promoting prosperity. It prevents the disruptive effects of fluctuating exchange rates on the international division of labor. However, from the very beginning, the system has flagrant design flaws that bring it down in the early 1970s: the acute problem areas are *balancing the balance of payments and providing international liquidity*.

Initially, America exports more than it imports. The foreign country therefore pays more dollars to America than Americans pay to the foreign countries. There is talk of a "dollar shortage." In fact, the countries that have reported a trade deficit with the US should have lowered their prices in order to increase their competitiveness at fixed exchange rates. But that was politically not desired. From 1959, the US balance of payments turns into a deficit: America imports more than it exports. The foreign countries begin to accumulate dollar assets. The dollar shortage turns into a "dollar glut." America had started to expand the US dollar money supply–mainly because of its belligerent foreign policy–without having a corresponding gold backing. This puts the US dollar under devaluation pressure and forces central banks in other countries to intervene in favor of the US dollar.

In the Bretton Woods system, they are forced to buy US dollars and pay for their purchases with newly created domestic currency. As a result, they import the Americans' inflationary monetary policy. The now rising money supply in their own country is causing prices to rise. In this way, the Americans cause an inflation of the entire system. In order for foreign countries to escape the devaluation of their own currency, the exchange rates are subsequently adjusted (realignments). For example, the German mark is revalued several times against the US dollar.

However, the US dollar is also beginning to depreciate against gold. As a result, eight major central banks–seven from Europe in addition to the US central bank–begin to hold the gold price at US $35 per troy ounce as early as November 1961 (London Gold Pool). They sell gold from their own reserves in order to counteract the rise in the price of the precious metal against the US dollar. But in vain. The markets drive the price of gold higher and higher, because the US dollar is inflationary. In March 1968, the central banks officially end their interventions in the gold market.

On August 15, 1971, US president Richard Nixon (1913–94) declared in a television speech that from now on the US dollar could no longer be redeemed for gold. The Americans had not been allowed to own physical gold since 1933, as President Franklin D. Roosevelt had forbidden it. Now the central banks of other countries can no longer exchange their dollar balances for gold. This unilateral decision not only removes the gold backing from the US dollar, but also turns all the world's major currencies into unbacked paper money, or fiat money.

The Bretton Woods system failed, because many countries were unwilling to unconditionally comply with the bidding of American inflationary policies. They escaped inflation by revaluing their own currencies. The voluntary solidarity that was supposed to hold the Bretton Woods system together proved too weak. Governments in many countries placed their domestic economic concerns above the obligations that arose from the international monetary system agreement, which Americans abused by inflating. The Bretton Woods system was finally terminated on March 2, 1973. Nevertheless, the US dollar strengthened its status as a world reserve currency.

The International Monetary Fund (IMF) amended its statutes in 1976. From then on, each IMF member country was free to choose its own exchange rate system, allowing flexible exchange rates. Exchange rate fluctuations were to be contained by "domestic stability" in the economies, no longer by central bank intervention in the foreign exchange markets. In principle, manipulation of exchange rates, intended to create advantages in foreign trade, was to be avoided.

As a result, a mixed exchange rate system emerges worldwide. Some countries (mainly developing countries) peg their currencies to other currencies or a basket of currencies at a fixed exchange rate. Still others agree fixed exchange rates with each other and flexible exchange rates with third parties (as is the case with the European Monetary Union, for example). Countries such as the United States, Japan, or the United Kingdom rely on flexible exchange rates.

The experience of the "dollar shortage" that emerged in the early years of the Bretton Woods system gave rise to a desire on the part of many countries to make their international liquidity independent of the US balance of payments situation. Until then, gold and US dollars had been the means of payment and currency reserves accepted worldwide. But by the end of the 1950s, the US had already begun to issue more and more US dollars that were not backed by gold. Under these conditions, it was foreseeable that the gold price in US dollars would come under appreciation pressure.

But raising the official gold price—a devaluation of the US dollar against gold, which was even explicitly provided for in the IMF agreement under certain conditions—was not politically opportune for several reasons:[90] (1) It would have benefited gold producers South Africa and the Soviet Union, one country an apartheid regime, the other the main opponent in the Cold War. (2) It would have discriminated against countries that in good faith held US dollars instead of gold. (3) It was feared that an increase in the price of gold would fuel speculation about further increases in the price of gold.

Since the official gold price was not to be raised, a further reserve currency was devised in addition to gold (which was increasingly in demand but limited in quantity) and the US dollar (which was less and less in demand and whose quantity was increasingly expanded): this was known as the *special drawing right* (SDR). The decision that the International Monetary Fund may issue special drawing rights was made in 1967. SDRs were first created in 1969 and issued to IMF participants. SDRs were allocated on the basis of the share of capital ("quota") held by each country in the IMF.

SDRs are not money but represent a claim against all IMF participating countries for foreign currencies. Specifically, this means that a country with a balance-of-payments deficit can convert its SDRs at the IMF into a desired participating country's national currency. The IMF then designates a country with a balance-of-payments surplus to provide the desired currency. The SDRs can be exercised under certain conditions by any IMF member country and have the potential to increase the global money supply; the SDR has therefore been aptly referred to as "global helicopter money."[91]

Originally, each SDR was worth exactly 0.888671 grams of gold. After the collapse of Bretton Woods in 1973, the definition was changed: from then on, the SDR was no longer an equivalent value of physical gold but corresponded to a "basket" of the main unbacked currencies. The composition of the SDR basket is reviewed every five years. Since October 1, 2016, the currency basket defining the SDR has consisted of US dollars, euros, Chinese renminbi, Japanese yen, and British pounds. The currencies are weighted as follows: US dollar, 41.73 percent; euro 30.93 percent, Chinese

---

[90] See Robert A. Mundell, "The International Monetary System and the Case for a World Currency" (lecture no. 12 of the Leon Koźmiński Academy of Entrepreneurship and Management and TIGER Distinguished Lecture Series, Warsaw, Poland, Oct. 23, 2003), p. 7; he cites five reasons here.

[91] Strictly speaking, the global money supply only increases if a country determined by the IMF to provide another country with an amount in its own currency expands its own money supply in order to do so.

renminbi 10.92 percent, Japanese yen 8.33 percent, and British pound, 8.09 percent. SDRs can only be held by the central banks of IMF member states and are used for payments between participating countries and toward the IMF. For example, the IMF can grant loans in the form of SDRs instead of national currencies, or it can replenish a country's scarce foreign reserves by granting SDRs. SDRs cannot be used directly on the foreign exchange markets. They must first be exchanged for a marketable currency.

The global financial and economic crisis of 2008-09 has given new impetus to political interest in the IMF. In April 2009, the G20 decided to *strengthen* the IMF by significantly expanding its ability to issue SDRs and create additional credit. Initially, it was decided to triple the IMF's freely available financial resources to a total of more than $750 billion and to increase the SDRs to the tune of around $250 billion; before that, the stock was only $33 billion.[92] Following a resolution on November 24, 2009, the IMF's financial resources were further increased to a total of $934 billion.

The inspiration for these decisions was the idea to turn the IMF into a "global rescue fund." However, according to the IMF agreement, it is the IMF's task to provide financial assistance for a country's balance of payments problems–an objective derived from the Bretton Woods system (which is actually no longer necessary in today's flexible exchange rate system). The purpose of SDR allocations is to meet a long-term need for additional foreign reserve assets. Now, however, the IMF has been provided with bilateral credit lines to increase its financial firepower in the short term.

The IMF–also because the scope of action of its leadership has been extended–therefore increasingly resembles a *world central bank* that can issue SDRs and also grant loans in national currencies. The SDR is therefore often seen as a precursor, a kind of nucleus, of a single world currency. From a purely technical standpoint, this view is not unfounded: it would only take a few decisions or actions to make the SDR a single world currency–proclaiming and enforcing *irrevocably* fixed exchange rates or merging national currencies with the SDR.

This idea inspired the creation of the euro at the beginning of 1999 and has already been tried out in practice. What today is praised as the

[92] See Deutsche Bundesbank, *Finanzierung und Repräsentanz im Internationalen Währungsfonds*, March 2010, pp. 57-58.

successful unification of monetary relations in Europe is to be interpreted quite differently from a logical point of view: the euro is the result of an effort to put an end to monetary diversity in Europe and to create a unified state currency. It was not left to the free-market forces to provide the desired unified money; instead it was promoted by state coercive measures and therefore also conceived as state fiat unified money. This will be explained in the following chapter.

CHAPTER 17

CAMPAIGN AGAINST CURRENCY CHOICE: THE EURO

Europe will be made through a currency, or it will not be made.[93]

— JACQUES RUEFF

The proponents of a "United States of Europe" realized at some point that the way to merge a multitude of nation-states into one central state could not be a direct one. The resistance of the populations concerned about their sovereignty was too great for this; this was explained in chapter 13. The objective therefore had to be achieved by other means. Democratic socialism therefore recommends a single currency for Europe, because it forces the nation-states to merge into a single central state, as it were—and this is due to the consequences that arise from this decision: the creation of a politicized single currency should be the compelling force for the unified state.

The decisive step was taken on January 1, 1999. On that day, the currencies of eleven nation-states—all of them unbacked paper currencies—were converted into a single currency, the euro. In addition to Belgium, Germany, Finland, France, Ireland, Italy, Luxembourg, the Netherlands, Austria, Portugal, and Spain, eight more countries eventually joined: Greece (2001), Slovenia (2007), Malta and Cyprus (2008), Slovakia (2009), Estonia (2011), Latvia (2014), and Lithuania (2015). The euro was declared the sole legal tender in all participating countries. The production monopoly for the euro is held by the European Central Bank (ECB).

It was a long and sometimes arduous path to the euro.[94] As early as 1969, a step-by-step plan to establish an economic and monetary union

[93] Jacques Rueff, "L'Europe se fera par la monnaie ou ne se fera pas," *in L'âge de l'inflation* (Paris: Payot, 1963), p. 128.

[94] See for example Arwed M. von Poser, *Europäische Währungsunion: Der Weg zum Euro-Kapitalmarkt*, 3d ed. (Stuttgart: Deutscher Sparkassen Verlag, 1998).

in Europe was drawn up (the Werner Plan). In its second and third stages, it was intended, *inter alia*, to make Europe's currencies fully convertible, liberalize capital movements across borders, reduce exchange rate fluctuations, and ultimately irrevocably set fixed parities between national currencies. In response to the end of the Bretton Woods system in the early 1970s, a European "snake in the tunnel" (EST) was launched. Its purpose was to limit exchange rate fluctuations. However, the first oil price crisis in 1973 and the associated economic consequences led many countries to withdraw from the EST.

A European unit of account (gold UA) had existed since the early 1950s. It was defined in gold, like the US dollar: 1/35th of an ounce of fine gold was equivalent to one US dollar. However, the European UA did not develop an independent profile and was not usable in transactions. After the IMF's SDR was redefined from gold to US dollars in mid-1974, the European UA was retroactively redefined on July 1, 1974, from gold to merely a basket of European currencies.

In 1979, the European Monetary System (EMS) was adopted as the successor to the EST. Like the EST before it, the EMS was intended to reduce exchange rate fluctuations and thus strengthen economic and monetary cooperation in Europe. The EMS provided that exchange rate fluctuations between the individual currencies were not to fluctuate more than ± 2.25 percent upward or downward around the central exchange rate parities—which were politically determined. Following the establishment of the EMS, the European UA was replaced by the ECU (European currency unit) on January 1, 1981.

The EMS was in many ways imperfect. For example, it provided for a mutual obligation to intervene. An example: if Italy inflated more strongly than Germany and therefore depreciated the Italian lira against the German mark, the Bank of Italy had to buy lira on the foreign exchange market and sell German marks. At the same time, the Bundesbank was required to buy lira and pay for them with (newly created) German marks. This led to a tightening of the money supply in Italy and an expansion of the money supply in Germany. Inflation was by tendency contained in Italy and increased in Germany. The EMS thus ensured that the inflation policies of one state had to be at least partially adopted by the other states.

In addition, the central bank whose currency depreciated had to have currency reserves in the revaluing currency—otherwise it would not have been able to fulfill its intervention obligations in the EMS. To this end, the

European Monetary Cooperation Fund (EMCF) was set up in 1973. It was to handle the necessary foreign exchange intervention within the framework of the then "European currency snake." Within the EMS, the EMCF was also responsible for managing the credit mechanism in the EMS mutual assistance agreement. The EMCF was dissolved in 1994 and became the European Monetary Institute (EMI), the forerunner of the ECB.

In the EMS, there was some realignment of currency parities: the change in exchange rates was occasionally allowed as an adjustment parameter to compensate for shifting competitiveness between the economies participating in the EMS. This was completely incompatible with the spirit of a system of fixed exchange rates. In 1992 there was a serious crisis: the monetary policy in the wake of German reunification caused inflation in Germany to rise. The Deutsche Bundesbank–which consistently geared its monetary policy toward domestic requirements–reacted with strong interest rate hikes.

The German central bank thus decided to fight domestic inflation, even if this would lead to tensions in the EMS. As a result, many of the currencies participating in the EMS were subject to devaluation speculation. The central banks concerned attempted to maintain their exchange rate parities by raising interest rates and intervening in foreign exchange markets. But in vain. On August 2, 1993, it was announced that the previously applicable exchange rate fluctuation margins from 4.5 percent were widened to 30 percent. Basically, this seemed to be the end of fixed exchange rates in Europe. After only a few weeks, however, the exchange rates of the major ERM (European Exchange Rate Mechanism) currencies (the German mark, the French and Belgian francs, the Dutch guilder, the Danish krone) had returned to the narrow fluctuation band that prevailed before the crisis. Following the EMS crisis, the exchange rate fluctuation margins were extended to ±15 percent. The idea was to reduce intervention pressure and speculative incentives.

Above all, the crisis of the British pound made it clear to everyone that a system of fixed exchange rates composed of national sovereign currencies is ultimately an extremely unstable affair. The pound was only included in the EMS in October 1990, at a rate of 2.95 German marks to the pound. On September 16, 1992, "Black Wednesday," there was massive speculation against the British currency. Then, the Bank of England raised its key interest rate twice. When the exchange rate did not stabilize, it announced its exit from the EMS that same evening. The pound fell below

2.35 marks. The British had preferred to devalue the pound in the hope of preventing high interest rates and a slowdown in their economy.

The sterling crisis drew attention to a special feature in the EMS: Germany was not only the economically largest and most populous participant, it was also one of the countries with the greatest (partly historically explainable) "dislike of inflation." If the other countries pursued an inflation policy that was not desired in Germany, they either had to abandon it or they had to reckon with a devaluation of their currency in the foreign exchange market. As long as the German mark's sovereignty remained in place, monetary policy in Europe could only be conducted with, but not against, Germany.

Under this condition, there were only two ways to achieve the political objective of monetary unification: (1) Germany would be allowed to determine monetary policy in Europe. This would have been technically possible if the other EU countries had renounced their own monetary policies and completely transferred their currency sovereignty to Germany. Politically, that was not desired. (2) The only alternative, therefore, was for the German mark to merge into a common currency–a currency which is issued by all countries, in a manner of speaking. And that's exactly how it happened.

In particular, two important decisions were necessary. *First*, national monetary sovereignty had to be abolished once and for all. This means that control over the domestic money supply, key interest rates and inflation had to be *irrevocably* transferred to a supranational central bank. A departure from this decision should no longer be possible. *Second*, the name of the national currency (German mark, French franc, Italian lira, etc.) had to disappear from people's minds, from daily business transactions. The new supranational currency had to have a name that replaced the names of the national currencies.

The path to the euro monetary union was designed entirely in this spirit. The EMS ended on December 31, 1998. On that day, the exchange rates of the countries participating in monetary union were fixed (on the basis of ECU parities) and on that basis they were irrevocably converted into the single currency, the euro, on January 1, 1999. The national central banks became branches of the ECB subject to instructions. The Governing Council, the supreme decision-making body of the ECB, has since determined the fate of monetary policy. The Governing Council of the ECB comprises all countries participating in the monetary union, with the weighting of "one country, one vote."[95]

In the run-up to the introduction of the euro, politicians tried to make the advantages and opportunities of monetary union and the single currency palatable to the public—while the costs of the single currency were mostly ignored or at least played down. A single currency would, it was said, bring fixed exchange rates. And this would increase planning security for companies with regard to foreign trade and cross-border investments. Individual countries could no longer gain unfair advantages by devaluing their currency.

Transaction costs would fall, especially for consumers and companies: it would no longer be necessary to constantly exchange one currency for another. In addition, there would be no costs for currency hedging. The improved price transparency would also be booked on the credit side of the single currency: without exchange rate fluctuations and without transaction and hedging costs, it would be easier to compare prices in different countries. This in turn would improve the ability to make economically meaningful decisions.

Last but not least, the European single currency is associated with the political desire to compete with the US dollar, the world's reserve currency. Having only a single currency in Europe would make it possible to create a large and liquid securities market. Such an achievement would make it more attractive for international investors to invest in Europe. This in turn would lower credit and capital costs and promote investment, production, and employment in the European community of states.

All these arguments are all very well. But they hide the fact that the introduction of the euro ultimately grew out of a different objective: states strive for power expansion and control. The domination of money plays a decisive, indispensable role in this. Every state strives to ensure that its money is used and to discourage, and, if necessary, to rigorously prevent, the use of alternative currencies (as they would arise in the free market). And if states are large and powerful enough, they will act out this urge not only on their own territory, but also internationally. In Europe, democratic socialism launched something at the beginning of 1999 that prior to that had long been considered impossible: eleven nations agreed to terminate their monetary sovereignty, gave up their right of self-determination in the choice of money, and submitted to a political supranational institution, the ECB.

[95] Germany thus has the same voting rights in the Governing Council as Luxembourg or Slovenia.

But even the introduction of the euro does not yet mean, of course, that international currency competition is eliminated. The euro countries and their ECB do not yet have a *carte blanche.* As long as the international capital market is open and the euro can be exchanged for other currencies, the euro competes with other currencies. For example, if the ECB were to pursue a monetary policy of high inflation, euro money holders would switch to less inflationary currencies as far as possible. As long as other currencies are still available to which euro holders can switch, inflationary policy in the eurozone is at least subject to certain limits.

But of course, the euro single currency is not the end of the story. In recent years it has become apparent that monetary policies in the currency areas have converged markedly. Not only are the state fiat currencies that exist internationally structured according to the same blueprint, but national monetary policies have also converged markedly. This is mainly due to the ever-closer cooperation between the central banks. Without exaggerating, one can speak of a worldwide *central bank cartel.* This is the subject of the next chapter.

MAKING ONE CURRENCY OUT OF MANY

The euro monetary union began on January 1, 1999, with eleven nations whose currencies were fixed to the euro on December 31, 1998, at predetermined irrevocable exchange rates (the "official parities")—and thus exchange rates were fixed once and for all between themselves.[96] The illustration below shows the exchange rate development of selected currencies (quoted in euros) since the early 1970s and, from the beginning of 1999, the exchange rate of the euro against the US dollar. If a line in the chart rises (falls), this means that the respective currency has depreciated (appreciated) against the US dollar. But how was it possible to convert the national currencies into the euro?

The central banks have forced through the politically desired *fixed* exchange rates in the market. As monopolists of money production, this was possible for them. Let us assume that the French franc depreciates against the German mark and falls below the

---

[96] See for example Thorsten Polleit, A. M. Poser, "Wieviel Euro für eine D-Mark?" in *Zeitschrift für das gesamte Kreditwesen* (14/1997).

politically desired exchange rate. The Bank of France then buys francs on the foreign exchange market and offers German marks for them. It can only do this if it has currency reserves in German marks or if it receives German marks from the Deutsche Bundesbank.

Selected exchange rates of the participating nations for the euro*

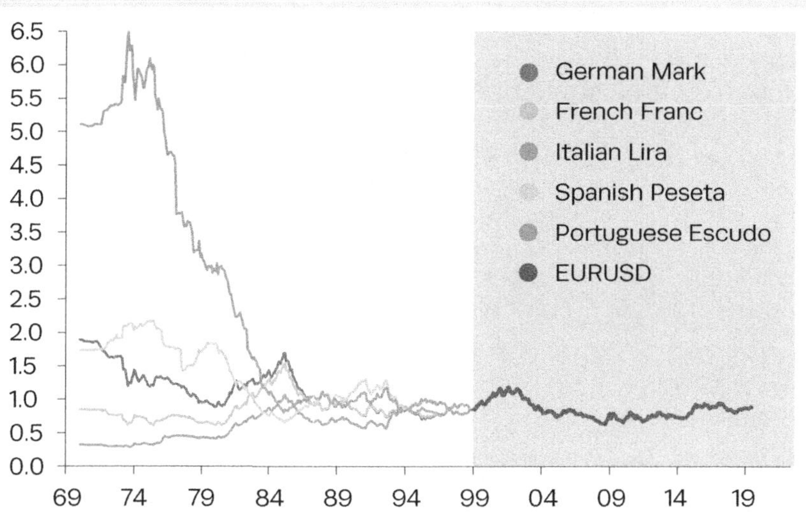

Source: Thomson Financial; own calculations.

* *Expressed as the number of national currencies to be paid for a US dollar.*

At the same time, the Bundesbank buys French francs and in return offers German marks. This "maneuvre" leads to a shortage of francs and an expansion of the supply of marks. In France there will be downward pressure and in Germany upward pressure on goods prices. If the central banks credibly assure the foreign exchange markets that they are willing to keep exchange rates at the politically desired level, they will be successful: The markets will then not speculate against the prices announced by the central banks.

CHAPTER 18

THE SECRET AND SINISTER POWER: THE WORLD CENTRAL BANK CARTEL

It is no coincidence that the century of total war coincided with the century of central banking.
— **RON PAUL**

Central banks have a long tradition of working together—and it usually happens unnoticed by the public.[97] The most obvious form of cross-border cooperation today is certainly the Bank for International Settlements (BIS). It was founded in 1930—mainly at the insistence of the governor of the Bank of England, Montagu Norman (1871-1950), and the president of the German Reichsbank, Hjalmar Schacht (1877-1970)—with its headquarters in Basel, Switzerland. The tasks of the BIS were to settle German reparations payments after the First World War and to promote cooperation between central banks.

As the "bank of central banks" and because of its not always publicly visible activities, especially during the Second World War, the BIS has always been the subject of critical observations and questions, as well as many a conspiracy theory.[98] This general skepticism toward the BIS is not unfounded. The history of central bank cooperation is undoubtedly shady. We only have to think of the granting of loans, which in the period of the "classical gold standard"—which can rightly be described as a

[97] An overview is provided by Gianni Toniolo and Claudio Borio, "One Hundred and Thirty Years of Central Bank Cooperation: A BIS Perspective" (BIS Working Paper No. 197, Feb. 24, 2006). One example is the Deutsche Golddiscontbank, which was founded in 1924 to promote German foreign trade and generate the necessary foreign exchange. This became possible because the Bank of England, at the request of the Reichsbank, was prepared to grant pound sterling loans to the new bank. See Andrew Boyle, *Montagu Norman: A Biography* (New York: Weybright and Talley, 1967), pp. 172–73.

[98] For example, see Adam LeBor, *Tower of Basel: The Shadowy History of the Secret Bank That Runs the World* (New York: Public Affairs, 2014).

phase of the "fake-" or "pseudo-gold standard"—occurred time and again between central banks.

Not only did the commercial banks issue more money by lending than they were able to redeem in gold, but the central banks did the same thing. It is no wonder that the markets have repeatedly expressed doubts that even the central banks were not in a position to fully redeem the money they spent in gold as promised. In order to prevent the cover on the whole fraud being blown, other central banks felt compelled to help out their central bank friends with loans in the event of a bank run; this was particularly pronounced, for example, in the time of the *gold exchange standard* in the late 1920s and early 1930s.[99]

It is therefore not surprising that the central banks—and the interest groups behind them—pushed for cooperation in times of the pseudo-gold standard. And so it is anything but astonishing that, in the age of fiat money, the urge of central banks to work together has not diminished, but has even increased,[100] because the worldwide fiat money system which exists in the world, and for which the central banks with their money monopoly are responsible, has produced a very specific dynamic of its own.

The coexistence of many state fiat currencies represents a kind of inhibited competitive situation. Every money holder can more or less easily exchange his or her home currency for other currencies; for example, he or she can change euros into US dollars and then hold them with US banks as a time deposit or money market certificate. At the same time, however, the states are very effective in ensuring—above all by means of tax laws—that in their respective territories only their own fiat money is used for payments, not other money or money that other states issue.

In every currency system—whether in a free market for money or in a juxtaposition of state fiat currencies—sooner or later the desire for a single currency takes off. Even in a global economy, it is economically advantageous for as many people as possible to use the same currency. In this to date hampered competition between state fiat currencies, the "greenback" is still ahead: the US dollar is the currency of the world's largest and most efficient economy; it is the currency of the largest and most liquid financial market.

---

[99] On the role of the Bank of England during this period, see Paul Einzig, *Montagu Norman: A Study in Financial Statesmanship* (London: K. Paul, Trench, Trubner, 1932), chap. 6.

[100] On this topic, see Toniolo, "One Hundred and Thirty Years of Central Bank Cooperation: A BIS Perspective," table 2, p. 4.

This is primarily due to the internationalization of the banking business, which has taken place in recent decades under the dominance of the US dollar. The financing of trade and financial transactions across borders, time zones, and currency areas is preferably carried out in US dollars. Export and import-oriented companies are also more dependent than ever on the US dollar. This is a reason why the Fed's monetary policy has a decisive influence on interest rates and liquidity conditions in the global financial markets.

In addition, the US dollar is the number one international reserve currency. In many other currency areas, the greenback serves as "base money." Whether the euro, Japanese yen, Chinese renminbi, Swiss franc, or British pound, all currencies today are more or less based on the US dollar. The US dollar and US government and bank debt denominated in US dollars are the most important foreign currency positions almost everywhere.

It is above all the banking business that is working in a special way toward a globally unified monetary policy and is thus preparing the ground for a single global currency. Banks are known to operate with a fractional reserve. This means that they hold only a very small fraction of their payment obligations to their customers, due at any time, in the form of central bank money.[101] In the worst-case scenario, they would not be able to fully meet their customers' disbursement requirements. In view of such latent illiquidity, banks are indeed vulnerable to loss of confidence.

This is particularly explosive in an increasingly internationalized financial world. After all, banks finance themselves not only in domestic currency, but also in foreign currencies. For example, euro banks need not only euros but also US dollars for their operations. Problems in a bank or problems in a currency area therefore have a rapid impact on the global banking system. The "contagion effects" therefore prompt the national central banks to coordinate particularly closely with each other and to act in unison, particularly in times of crisis.

This was unmistakably evident in the financial and economic crisis that began in 2007. As early as December 2007, the US Federal Reserve concluded a liquidity swap agreement in US dollars. In the course of a liquidity swap, for example, the Fed lends US dollar balances to the ECB.

[101] In March 2019, for example, the euro banks' sight liabilities, which are due at any time, amounted to €7,281 trillion. However, the balances held by the euro banks at the ECB—which could be exchanged for cash—amounted to only €1,972 trillion.

The ECB can lend the received US dollar balances to its domestic banks, which are no longer receiving US dollars on the credit markets. Consequently, by means of liquidity swap agreements, central banks are in a position to prevent payment defaults by banks engaged in the international market for foreign currency loans.[102]

CREATING MONEY OUT OF NOTHING WITH MONEY OUT OF NOTHING

Let us assume that euro banks have taken up debt in US dollars in order to be able to grant a loan in US dollars. Now the loans taken out by the banks are due. The banks have prepared themselves to refinance their maturing loans with new loans. But unexpectedly, a crisis breaks out and the banks find no more investors to lend them new US dollars. The banks thus run the risk of becoming insolvent. The ECB can provide the banks with unlimited amounts of euros, but not US dollars. However, if the ECB has access to a liquidity swap agreement with the US Federal Reserve, it is in a position to avert the insolvency of the euro banks in US dollars: The Fed lends the ECB the desired US dollar amount, and the ECB lends the greenbacks to the euro banks. A simple example can illustrate this.

ASSETS	FED		LIABILITIES
Deposit with the ECB (¬)	+100	Deposit of the ECB ($)	+110
			-110
		Deposits of euro banks ($)	+110

ASSETS	ECB		LIABILITIES
Deposits with the Fed ($)	+110	Deposits of the Fed (¬)	+100
	-110		
Credit to euro banks ($)	+110		

ASSETS	EURO AREA BANKING SECTOR		LIABILITIES
Deposit with the Fed ($)	+110	Liabilities vis-a-vis the ECB ($)	+110

[102] Further central banks were subsequently included in the scope of the US dollar liquidity swap agreement: the Reserve Bank of Australia, Banco Central do Brasil, the Bank of Canada, Danmarks Nationalbank, the Bank of England, the Bank of Japan, the Bank of Korea, Banco de Mexico, the Reserve Bank of New Zealand, Norges Bank, the Monetary Authority of Singapore, and Sveriges Riksbank. In November 2011, the Fed also entered into foreign currency liquidity swap agreements with the Bank of Canada, the Bank of England, the Bank of Japan, the European Central Bank, and the Swiss National Bank. This ensured that US banks had easy access to foreign currencies. On October 31, 2013, a brief press release was issued on the subject: the central banks announced that they had converted their existing liquidity swap agreements, which had *previously been limited in time*, into *open-ended* agreements.

(1) The ECB "draws" its swap line as granted to it by the Fed. This means that it sells to the Fed a euro amount (e.g., €100 billion), which it creates "out of nothing," at the given EUR/USD exchange rate (e.g., 1.00). In return it receives a corresponding US dollar amount (in this case $100 billion), which the Fed also creates "out of nothing." (2) The ECB undertakes to repurchase the €100 billion in the future (say, in three months) at the unchanged exchange rate.

An exchange rate risk is thus excluded. The ECB lends the US dollars to the banks on terms (interest rate, collateral, maturity, etc.) which it can determine itself. Consequently, the ECB, or the euro taxpayer, is liable to the Fed for the US dollar amount it has lent to the euro banks. The ECB and the euro taxpayers become debtors of the Fed. At the end of the liquidity swap, the ECB also pays the Fed the interest income it has earned from lending US dollars to the banks. The Fed does not pay interest on the euro amount it has received from the ECB. The Fed undertakes not to invest the euro amount and to hold it in a current account with the ECB. Economically, the liquidity swap agreement is a money creation out of nothing, based on money created out of nothing.

The liquidity swap agreements reveal the cartelization of the central banks, which de facto enforces the maintenance of the fiat money system. As a reminder, a cartel forms at the national level between central banks and domestic commercial banks. In this way, commercial banks are enabled—with the express approval of the state—to create money out of nothing by granting loans. The domestic central bank holds its protective hand over the financial institutions that operate with a fractional reserve and serves the banks as lender of last resort, thus ensuring that the systemically relevant banks in particular remain solvent at all times.

At the international level, a similar cartel of national central banks emerges. The fiat money system not only causes crises at the national, but also at the international level: the increasing trade and capital links between the national economies are ultimately financed with national fiat funds. And because economies are increasingly interdependent, especially through bank-financed credit links, national central banks must also be increasingly willing to help each other protect themselves: defaults at the national level can all too quickly trigger defaults at the international level.

This protection assistance not only involves the case-by-case coordination of policy measures between central banks. Under the heading of *technical central bank cooperation*, it has long since taken on a systematic, permanent character. The central banks maintain broad-based training and experience platforms with which the central bank staff in the various currency areas can be brought into line with each other in terms of expertise and, above all, monetary policy. This strengthens the ability and willingness of central banks to extend their cooperation; it facilitates cartel formation and makes cartelization *into something natural.*

But even the closest monetary policy cooperation between the central banks remains far behind the (monetary) political influence and control possibilities that a global central bank with its own single global currency would offer. Monetary cooperation between still sovereign states, based on voluntarism, is a fragile and unreliable affair. Let us recall the example of the liquidity swap agreements. The Fed takes a credit risk here when lending US dollars to the ECB: the ECB might not be able to repay the loan amount. The US Federal Reserve therefore holds the US taxpayers liable. It is they who must answer for the Fed's losses.

As long as the national central banks only have a mandate to conduct monetary policy for the domestic economy, there is a possibility that international rescue operations such as liquidity swap agreements could come under public criticism. Angry citizens and those elected by them are against subsidizing foreign banks. The central bank councils could counter this by saying that liquidity swaps, which supply foreign banks with domestic currency, would help fend off an even greater crisis, which would then also affect the domestic economy. But what if the electorate cannot be convinced?

There is no doubt that it will be difficult at this stage to politically convince voters in the various countries of the world to exchange their own currency for a supranational currency. This statement may apply in "normal times," but not necessarily in "times of crisis." In times of crisis, the scope for political leeway and action grows immensely. Financial and economic crises in particular have repeatedly proved to be a particularly fertile breeding ground for popularizing the idea of a world currency. As early as the 1930s, Fritz Machlup (1902–1983) wrote: "In times when the procurement of foreign means of payment is associated with difficulties, many businesspeople, who value highly the advantage of a foreign trade that is as unimpeded as possible, repeatedly raise the question of why a single world currency has not yet been introduced."[103]

The compelling solution for the democratic socialists is to merge the many national fiat funds into a single fiat world currency, which is then controlled by an all-powerful world central bank: in this way, a global fiat money system can be established with the greatest possible stability—a money system that can be perfectly controlled by the state, that exploits the inflationary potential for state financing to the greatest possible extent, and that contains the financial and economic crises that it inevitably causes in the best possible way. Is it, then, surprising that a whole series of concrete proposals have already been made on how to create a (fiat) world currency? Some of these proposals are presented in the following chapter.

[103] Machlup, *Führer durch die Krisenpolitik*, p. 160.

CHAPTER 19

PROPOSALS FOR A WORLD CURRENCY: BANCOR, UNITAS, US DOLLAR, INTOR, LIBRA

To get the full benefits of the monetary union, countries might want to have a currency reform that would make the national franc, or lira, or peso equivalent to one INTOR.
– **ROBERT MUNDELL**

The Bretton Woods system, which lasted from 1945 to 1973,[104] was based on two proposals: the *Keynes Plan* and the *White Plan* (see chapter 16). Both had the goal of creating a single world currency for the period after the Second World War. It was obvious in the Keynes Plan. But the White Plan also tended in this direction. It is instructive to first familiarize oneself with these two proposals—especially with the question of how (from a purely technical point of view) a world currency could be established in the future.

In September 1941, the economist John Maynard Keynes submitted a proposal to the British Treasury to establish a currency union, which he called the International Clearing Union (ICU). According to the Keynes Plan, the ICU's central task is to issue the international means of payment called *bancor*. The bancor is defined in gold. The currencies of the countries participating in the ICU are fixed against the bancor with a fixed parity. This creates a system of fixed exchange rates. Exchange rate

[104] In August 1971, the US government ended the gold redeemability of the US dollar. In March 1973, the G10 decided that the six members of the European Community should provide their currencies with fixed exchange rates and henceforth have a flexible exchange rate against the US dollar. In a way, this marked the real end of the Bretton Woods system.

adjustments *vis-à-vis* bancor are possible under certain conditions. Each participating country receives bancor credit by transferring its own gold reserves to the ICU. It is indeed possible for a country to obtain bancor against gold. But subsequently it cannot exchange the bancor received from the ICU back into gold. Seen in this light, the bancor is designed as a "mousetrap": once you're inside, you can't get out.

The total bancor quantity that the ICU can dispose of is determined on the basis of the foreign trade of all participating countries. Keynes recommends the following formula for determining the initial bancor supply: the sum of a country's exports and imports on average over the last three years before the outbreak of war. Under the Keynes Plan, participants grant each other book credits. For example, if country *A* achieves a trade surplus (i.e., exports exceed imports) over country *B* (which imports more than exports), the ICU grants country *A* a bancor credit, and country *B* a bancor loan. However, there is a limit on the overdraft on the bancor account: 25 percent of a country's quota of the previous year.

In this way, the ICU enables international trade to continue even if the importing countries have to finance the goods on credit. The ICU acts de facto as a supranational central bank. It issues its own gold-backed currency, which can be used for international trade. Although countries with a trade surplus temporarily receive bancor credit balances with the ICU, countries with a trade deficit are granted bancor loans. However, the ICU should ensure that there are no countries with trade surpluses or deficits in the long term. The Keynes Plan essentially aims to remove the dependence of international trade on the gold standard—so that countries with little gold (such as the UK) are not forced to restore their international competitiveness through falling commodity prices (deflation).

Unlike the Keynes Plan, the White Plan does not seek to establish a de facto supranational central bank that issues its own book money and grants credit and loans to countries. Rather, it provides for the creation of a fund to which the member states make payments according to their quota before they can draw on loans to finance balance of payments problems. The quota of a country is determined by gold and foreign exchange reserves, national income and foreign trade volume. Fifty percent of this quota must be paid in gold (12.5 percent), national currency (12.5 percent), and debt securities (25 percent).

Under the White Plan, the credit balances of the participating countries are reported in a uniform unit of account called *unitas* (1 unitas equates to 8.88687 grams of fine gold and thus 10 US dollars). The fund determines the parities of the national exchange rates with unitas. This results in fixed exchange rates. Their changes are only allowed in the case of fundamental external imbalances. In contrast to the Keynes Plan, the White Plan does not formally provide for an expansion of international liquidity. On the contrary, a country can only receive payment from the fund to finance balance-of-payments deficits in accordance with its quota.

The ideas of the White Plan prevailed in the Bretton Woods system. But they were not enough to create a single world currency. When the system failed and ended in the early 1970s, a worldwide monetary system followed that had never existed in monetary history before: all the world's major currencies are unbacked paper money whose exchange rates fluctuate more or less freely among themselves. This has repeatedly prompted the critique from many (mainstream) economists that such a global currency system would be detrimental to the increase in prosperity. Why is that?

Freely floating *nominal* exchange rates do not necessarily ensure that the correct real exchange rate is always achieved. Fluctuations in exchange rates may disturb the balance between economies, to the extent that it is determined by different price levels. The reason: in the short term, exchange ratios between the national currencies usually change faster and more strongly than the prices of goods and wages. If this is the case, the global division of labor will be disrupted, as it will no longer be ensured that international production takes place where it can be done at the lowest cost.

DETERMINING THE CORRECT EXCHANGE RATE

The purchasing power parity theory is often used to explain the exchange rate between two currencies. It states that the prices of the same good in different currencies must be equal to each other. Consider this equation:

$$P = P^* / W$$

P (P^*) is the price of the goods in domestic currency (foreign currency). W is the *nominal* exchange rate, expressed as the price of the domestic currency in units of the foreign currency (as is usual, for example, for euro rates). A nominal appreciation (depreciation) of the domestic currency is reflected in an appreciation (depreciation) of W.

If the nominal exchange rate between home and abroad is fixed once and for all at, for example, $W = 1$, then the prices of goods must be equal to each other: $P = P^*$.

In addition to the nominal exchange rate, there is also a *real* exchange rate (R). It results from this equation:

$$R = W \times (P/P^*)$$

Let us assume that P = 100 and P^* = 200. For R to be 1 (i.e., the purchasing power parity applies), W must be 2. And let us assume that domestic inflation rises so that $P = 120$. For the purchasing power parity to continue to apply, the exchange rate of the domestic currency must devalue against the foreign currency, in this case to $W = 1.67$.

The economic criticism of fluctuating exchange rates cannot be dismissed—and democratic socialism with its claim to worldwide validity knows how to make use of it. The demand that it derives from its criticism is that we should create a single world currency under the sovereignty of the international community. The financial and economic crises that have become increasingly severe in recent years are grist for the mills of this proposal. The creation of a single world currency is being expedited on the grounds that the international coordination of monetary policies must be promoted and intensified in order to effectively prevent new crises. Many plans have already been drafted for the implementation of the project.

The American economist Richard N. Cooper (b. 1934) published the essay “A Monetary System for the Future” in 1984, which received great attention. Cooper argues that the global division of labor will intensify in the future—especially through technical innovations—and that for this reason changes in real exchange rates could disrupt global production and employment to a particularly large extent. This is why he calls for an exchange rate system that ensures reliable fixed exchange rates—which is the case when only one currency is used worldwide.

Cooper argues that nation-states should give up their monetary sovereignty and transfer it to a global central bank, the Global Bank of Issue, which should be responsible for global monetary policy. Monetary policy decisions would be made by a governing board in which the states are represented by their finance ministers (according to their economic weight in world production). The World Central Bank would produce its own money by buying (monetizing) debt securities of member states and/or by discounting, in the course of open market operations, acceptable debt securities offered to it on the initiative of commercial banks.

The single world currency issued by the World Central Bank could be created from any already established unbacked paper currency. Cooper sees the US dollar as the natural candidate. But the world currency could also be an artificial (synthetic) unit (such as the IMF's special drawing right) to which the public would have to become accustomed (as it once became accustomed to a metric number system). What is decisive for Cooper is that the world currency would no longer be in the hands of the national governments, but in the hands of a supranational institution.

At the time his proposal was published, Cooper himself described his idea of world currency as "too radical" to be implemented in the near future. It would have been necessary to implement it over a period of twenty-five years (that would have been by 2010 at the latest) to prevent a relapse into a state of global trade and capital movement barriers. However, Cooper identifies two major problems in trying to create a single world currency. First, not all countries in the world would have been able to participate because of the existence of the Iron Curtain at the time. And second, (acceptance) problems could be expected in the developed economies if representatives of autocratic regimes were represented in the decision-making body of the World Central Bank.

In addition, Cooper sees the need to make the general population familiar with the plan to end national currency sovereignty and transfer it to a supranational authority. He sees an important step on the way to a single world currency in the formation of a (leading) group of countries—the US, Canada, Japan, and the European states—which are initially to begin to reduce the exchange rate fluctuations of their currencies.

If *N* countries in the group *N-1* stabilize exchange rates, there is a remaining degree of freedom: a currency can then serve as an anchor that determines the money supply in the group as a whole. But which currency should be the anchor. If it is a fiat currency (such as the US dollar), the welfare of all other currencies depends on this anchor fiat currency. The United States, as the undisputed leading-currency country, did not adhere to the rules of the Bretton Woods system, and abused it for its own purposes in an inflationary manner, which led to the failure of this currency arrangement in the early 1970s.

With his proposal, Cooper did not really break new ground, and basically did not go beyond the legacy of the Bretton Woods system—although he also saw the option of creating the world currency as unbacked paper money as a possible solution. The other is a proposal for the creation of a single world currency by the Canadian economist Robert Mundell (b. 1932). Like Cooper, Mundell, who was awarded the Nobel Prize for Economics in 1999, takes into account the fact that fluctuating exchange rates disrupt the international division of labor. The constant ups and downs on the foreign exchange markets do not ensure that the exchange rates are always the right ones in *real* terms: a system of fluctuating exchange rates is not optimal; a system of fixed exchange rates, especially in the form of a single world currency, is preferable.

In order to achieve the global currency, Mundell proposes to first stabilize the exchange rates between the world's major currencies—the US dollar, the euro, the Japanese yen, the British pound, and possibly also the Chinese renminbi. To this end, monetary policymakers in these currency areas should agree to keep inflation low. Then there were to be agreed bandwidths within which exchange rates could fluctuate. When exchange rates reached the upper or lower bounds, central banks would have to intervene in the foreign exchange markets to maintain exchange rates. This would reduce fluctuations in real exchange rates.

Of course, Mundell recognizes that such a system of fixed exchange rates is vulnerable because some participants have the incentive and the option of leaving. An example should illustrate this. Suppose the Fed and the ECB set a 1:1 exchange rate between the US dollar and the euro. Then the ECB begins to pursue an inflation policy. The euro becomes less attractive to investors. As a result, they increasingly offer euros on the foreign exchange market and demand US dollars. The US dollar begins to appreciate against the euro.

In order to keep the exchange rate at 1:1, the ECB must buy euros on the foreign exchange market and sell US dollars. This will reduce the euro money supply and domestic inflation. The Fed must buy euros against issuance of new US dollars, thereby increasing its domestic money supply and thus its domestic inflation. This in turn lowers the relative attractiveness of the US dollar, and the exchange rate moves back to the agreed ratio of 1:1. As a result, the fixed exchange rate is maintained, but only because the Fed is willing to participate in part in the ECB's inflation policy.

Such a system of fixed exchange rates, participation in which is voluntary and which allows a participant to leave it again, cannot be sustained if the participants want to pursue different inflation policies or different monetary policy objectives concurrently. Mundell therefore considers it necessary to arrive at a global currency unit (initially *not* a single global currency) via an "intermediate step" which reduces exchange rate fluctuations. Specifically, Mundell's proposal provides for three stages.

Stage 1: transition to a regime of stable exchange rates. It is characterized by intervention obligations on the part of the participating central banks to establish and defend the fixed exchange rates in the market. Stage 2: creation of a core group of countries (such as the United States, the eurozone countries, Japan, the United Kingdom, and possibly China) that fix exchange rates at certain parities and conduct a coordinated, common monetary policy in order to meet exchange rate targets. Stage 3: a global world currency is created. Mundell suggests the name INTOR: *INT* is the abbreviation for *international* and *OR*, the French word for *gold*. The currencies of the participating countries are pegged to the INTOR at a fixed (but possibly variable) exchange rate. The US dollar, euro, Japanese yen and Chinese renminbi remain the same in name and are freely convertible into the INTOR.

Subsequently, other countries have the option of tying their exchange rates to the INTOR as well. This too allows their exchange rates to be fixed against all other currencies. However, one important question remains: What kind of money should the INTOR be? Mundell assigns the IMF board the task of officially determining the currency basket for the INTOR–initially consisting of the US dollar, euro, and Japanese yen. The INTOR in this form would be a currency basket, an index very similar to the SDR issued by the IMF. Consequently, as with the SDR, the exchange value of the INTOR would be determined by the central banks of the participating currencies. As monetary history and economic theory show, this is *not* a recipe for good money.

In addition, INTOR exhibits a well-known problem: if there are mutual intervention obligations between the central banks to stabilize the exchange rate, the inflationary policy of one country can force all other countries into "a policy of inflation" or "inflationary policy." According to Mundell, the IMF board of directors, which he recommends as a monetary policy body, would also be allowed to change the composition of the INTOR and the weights of the individual currencies in the it. The possibility of making such discretionary decisions arouses political desire and could sometimes significantly change the market or exchange value of the INTOR.

Mundell also hints at the possibility of backing the INTOR with gold. What do we make of that? If the INTOR is an expression of a certain quantity of fine gold, then a gold foreign exchange standard would again be created à la Bretton Woods. The system would be vulnerable to changes to the gold INTOR ratio. The latter would be left to the political arbitrariness of the IMF board of directors. In contrast to the Bretton Woods system, not a single country (the United States) would not decide on the gold INTOR exchange ratio, but the country representatives represented in the IMF body according to their economic strength. But would that really be an arrangement from which one can expect reliable money for the world? Hardly.

Mundell's remarks ultimately show that an INTOR, alongside which the national currencies would continue to exist and circulate, can only be an intermediate step. For the maximum benefit which a monetary community with fixed exchange rates provides, and which above all the democratic socialists strive for, will only be achieved when, in the course of a currency reform, the national currencies are merged into the INTOR—just as the European currencies have been integrated in the euro. This illustrates the line of development intended for INTOR: an initial world currency that exists alongside national currencies should ultimately become a single world currency.

The concepts presented so far for the creation of a world currency originate from the idea that states should provide the money of the world. A *private initiative* comes from the American internet giant Facebook. On closer inspection, however, it is merely a matter of "saddling" a unit of account onto the existing fiat currencies. But one thing at a time. In June 2019, the company announced that it wanted to offer its customers a global high-tech currency and infrastructure in 2020. According to Facebook, many people around the world are to have easy and inexpensive access to the monetary and financial system. The new blockchain-based money is called "Libra." The heart of the project is the Libra Association (LA). This nongovernmental association based in Geneva, Switzerland, was originally supported by founding members such as eBay, Facebook, Mastercard, PayPal, Spotify, Uber, Visa, and other renowned companies that were meant to be responsible for the operation and further development of Libra. Is Libra the way to a world currency?[105]

If many people prefer to settle their payments in Libra in the future and no longer in national fiat money, the Libra could well rise to acquire the status of world money. But is that realistic? The original idea was that Libra are created by people depositing US dollars or euros with the LA, which then grants the depositors a corresponding sum of Libra in a digital wallet. This sum may be used for payment purposes via the computer, smartphone, credit card, or WhatsApp and Messenger, Facebook's chat services. Technically, it would be a crypto-money banknote covered by a basket of official fiat funds (such as US dollars, euros, and the like). Consequently, the reliability of the Libra would stand and fall with the quality of the underlying fiat currencies. The Libra will be inflationary money to the extent that the US dollar, the euro, etc., are inflated by the central banks; it will lose its purchasing power in step with the official paper currencies. In an extreme case, i.e., if the official currencies were to go under, the Libra would also be lost. So Facebook money is not a real alternative to the official fiat money, at best an easier way to use it.

The idea of the Libra inventors is to keep the paid-in fiat sums of money as a "reserve": the aim is to ensure that the conversion of Libra into national fiat money is possible at any time, by holding the fiat funds paid in as deposits with banks or by using them to buy interest-bearing securities. The result is a kind of "partial reserve." The Libra is thus not only as inflationary as the fiat money, it also bears the risk of default—which will happen when the LA makes bad investment decisions or the credit market situation prevents the Libra owners' exchange wishes for the desired fiat money from being completely fulfilled.

With the investment of the reserve, Facebook and its comrades in arms hope to generate interest income. But that will be difficult. The central banks have already pushed interest rates to extremely low levels, and there is no sign of a move away from this monetary policy. And if the monetary authorities allocate a negative interest rate to the bank balances, the Libra customers will also be affected: if the LA is asked to pay for the reserve, it will have to pass on the costs to the Libra owners. Whoever then holds Libra will have to pay for it. It is a mistake to believe that the Libra might open up a way to evade bad fiat money.

---

[105] Meanwhile, Vodafone, Visa, eBay, and PayPal, among others, have withdrawn from the project.

The Libra project does not aim to provide better-quality money to people around the world. The fact that the Libra accounts and payments are to be represented using a private (permissioned) blockchain does not change this. The Libra project of Facebook and friends is an entrepreneurial attempt to earn money in the global market for payment services (and later perhaps also in the market for loans)—and to get hold of as much data as possible. If the goal is to offer people in this world a better, form of money, the LA would have to do the obvious: offer a 100 percent gold-backed Libra. But who knows, maybe this will be the next step, initiated by Facebook, Amazon or any other company.

The Libra would to some extent be a digital coupon for national fiat currencies. Its design can therefore be compared with the IMF's SDR. Like the SDR, the Libra represents a basket of national fiat currencies. While in the SDR it is the IMF that decides which national fiat currencies will be included in the SDR and what weight will be given to them, in the Libra it would be the LA that would be making all these decisions. If the Libra found great acceptance worldwide, the LA would grow into an extremely powerful position: it would become the depository for a huge amount of money or, if the LA invests the money in debt securities, a gigantic investor with dominant market influence.

Therefore, it is not surprising that the Facebook money concept has called the central banks into action. In view of overt resistance on the part of states, central banks, and state regulatory bodies, the LA reduced its ambition in April 2020. Most importantly, the association abandoned its original plan to create a global "stablecoin" directly tied to a fiat currency basket. It now plans to release several stablecoins—each of them will be backed by a fiat currency, such as the US dollar, the euro, and the British pound. There will also be a multi-fiat currency Libra "coin," a composite of the single-currency stablecoins. The LA also abandoned its plan make the Libra blockchain a "permissionless blockchain" (so it actually seems to be difficult to call it a blockchain in the true sense of the word). What is more, the LA wishes its network to provide a clear path to seamlessly integrate central bank digital currencies (CBDCs) as they become available. Therefore, the Libra project—at least for now—succumbs to the states and their central banks' claim a monopoly in money production.

In August 2019, the then governor of the Bank of England, Mark Carney, came forward with the idea that a "network of central banks" should launch a digital currency.[106] His argument: the dollar is used to settle at least half of international trade transactions, a sum five times larger than US imports (through which foreigners can earn US dollars). In order to reduce the dependence of the world economy on the US dollar, he proposed a diversified multipolar financial system that provides a substitute reserve currency through new technologies. According to Carney, a private initiative à la the Libra project is not suitable for this. He posed the telling question of whether such a new *synthetic hegemonic currency* (SHC) might not be best provided by the public sector, perhaps through a network of central bank digital currencies (CBDCs). It could be built on the blueprint of the Libra project, but it would be entirely in the hands of the central banks.

The supporters of a state-controlled world currency are not only to be found in Western countries. In March 2009, the then governor of the People's Bank of China, Zhou Xiaochuan, spoke out in favor of replacing the US dollar as the world's reserve currency with a revaluation of the special drawing rights (SDRs) issued by the International Monetary Fund.[107] Zhou's call (on behalf of China's Communist Party) for a reform of the global monetary system was aimed at reducing the world's dependence on the US dollar and achieving a global currency that no longer depends on credit-based national currencies. Since then, no concrete proposals have been submitted to the public—however, the Chinese renminbi was included in the SDR basket in 2016.

At this point, the digital currencies that central banks could issue in the future deserve a brief mention.[108] For example, the Swedish Riksbank is considering offering an "ekrona" which would compete with Swedish kronor in the form of cash and sight deposits at commercial banks. There are similar projects in China, Russia, and Venezuela. If digital central bank money is accepted, payment transactions will be transferred from the balance sheets of commercial banks to the balance sheet of the central bank. The central bank then obtains the perfect insight into who pays and receives what, when, where, and for what; it becomes the omniscient Big Brother.

[106] See Mark Carney, "The Growing Challenges for Monetary Policy in the Current International Monetary and Financial System" (speech given at Jackson Hole Symposium, Jackson Hole, WY, Aug. 23, 2019), p. 15: "As a consequence, it is an open question whether such a new Synthetic Hegemonic Currency (SHC) would be best provided by the public sector, perhaps through a network of central bank digital currencies."

[107] See Xiaochuan Zhou, "Reform the International Monetary System," *BIS Review* 41 (2009): esp. 2.

[108] Representatives of the Bank of England dealt with this issue at an early stage. See Ben Broadbent, "Central Banks and Digital Currencies" (speech given at the London School of Economics, London, Mar. 2, 2016), www.bis.org/review/r160303e.pdf.

There is a reason why most central banks are still reluctant to make digital central bank money available for all: it would constitute fierce competition for the deposit business of commercial banks. And the central banks need the commercial banks to expand the money supply through lending. Under prevailing conditions, money supply growth through lending requires equity capital, and in most currency areas this is still largely provided by private investors. Issuing digital central bank money to all would weaken commercial banks, and, politically, this is currently not desired in most Western countries. In China, on the other hand, things are different: Chinese banks are directly or indirectly in the hands of the state, and the obstacles to introducing digital central bank money for all are correspondingly low there.

But back to the core question: Can a fiat world currency (such as the SHC) be established voluntarily? The nations that have relatively better (i.e., less inflationary) fiat currencies have an incentive to exit if participation in the world currency leads to unacceptably high inflation in their home country; a voluntary cartel of central banks, which would be necessary to unify world monetary policy, would therefore be unstable. A fiat world currency could probably only be created if—as in the case of the euro—the nation-states or their voters were prepared to once and for all hand over *self-determination over their money* to a central body within the network of national central banks, i.e., a world central bank.

From a technical point of view, this is relatively easy to achieve, namely by merging the national fiat currencies into a single fiat currency. This step is likely to be opposed with considerable reservations on the part of the nation-states at present. However, the resistance is not guaranteed. For under democratic socialism, the states or the majority of voters will not be fundamentally averse to monetary centralization. One line of development could be that large countries first adopt a common currency and smaller countries follow the example with a time lag.

But is it realistic to expect that the United States, the European Union or the eurozone, Japan, the United Kingdom, China, and Russia will ultimately join forces and create a single fiat world currency? The likelihood that something like this will happen is probably greater than it may seem at first glance. For if democratic socialism continues to expand under the leadership of an *oligarchized party democracy*, the interests of the states will also converge ever closer together. The past decade has shown all too clearly how, for example, the interests of the Communist Party in Beijing and those of the democratic socialist governments, the "establishment," "big business," "Wall Street," the "Davos elite" have already joined forces quite harmoniously.[109]

It is not only the Communist leadership in China that is striving to gain total control over its citizens and entrepreneurs.[110] In the United States and Europe, for example, the overly powerful state–the "deep state"–is also on the advance, favored by the immense technical progress in the possibilities of control, the ever closer convergence of *surveillance business* and *surveillance state*, which is not sufficiently sanctioned by the electorate. Civil and entrepreneurial freedoms in the Western world are thus increasingly dwindling in favor of state influence and expansion of power.

In the Western world, *political ideology* has become increasingly unified in recent decades and has become more and more narrowed down to *democratic socialism*. It is essentially an ideology that is hostile to freedom, glorifies the state, and therefore does not differ categorically from an authoritarian regime such as the one in China. We should not be deceived: for the democratic socialists, the democratic element is merely a means to an end. With its help they want to gain dominion: socialism is the goal, and it is to be helped to victory by parliamentary means. Once it has been established, however, the socialists will of course no longer grant their opponents democratic freedoms. The Chinese coercive regime can certainly be understood as an expression of the endpoint toward which democratic socialism is working and which–as was shown in the preceding chapters–it can probably only achieve with a single world currency.

New financial and economic crises will strengthen the tendency of the political forces to create a fiat world currency. Just think of the social "hardships" that arise when the financial and economic system is severely shaken, when recession, loan defaults, bank failures, and social unrest spread in many countries. In times of such great distress, the willingness of people to accept unusual measures grows, of course, if these promise "rescue from hardship." For the democratic socialists,

---

[109] However, the collaboration was severely disrupted by the inauguration of US President Donald J. Trump in January 2017.

[110] It should be mentioned that the expectation that China would break away from the dictatorship of the Communist Party and turn to democracy has not yet been met. Rather the opposite seems to be the case: in March 2018, the National People's Congress, the Chinese pseudo-parliament, secured a lifetime rule for President Xi Jinping. Deng Xiaoping had already separated party and government in 1982 and he had also introduced a regulation according to which there was to be a change of leadership every ten years. Xi Jinping's empowerment must awaken memories of despotic rule.

such crises are "windows of opportunity" that can be used to initiate policies that would not be possible under normal circumstances; it was not for nothing that Karl Marx and Friedrich Engels saw "trade crises" as the prerequisite for the transition to communism.[111] From this perspective, a major financial and economic crisis would be a circumstance in which to give the go-ahead for a single fiat world currency. However, the following chapter shows how problematic this is.

[111] See Karl Marx and Friedrich Engels, *Manifest der Kommunistischen Partei: Mit Vorreden von Karl Marx und Friedrich Engels* (*The Communist Manifesto*) (Hamburg: Phönix Verlag, 1946).

CHAPTER 20

THE DYSTOPIA: A SINGLE WORLD FIAT CURRENCY

When governments fear the people, there is liberty. When the people fear the government, there is tyranny.

– **THOMAS JEFFERSON**

What would be so problematic if the states were to come together and create a single world currency? That's a perfectly valid question. As already mentioned several times, from a purely economic point of view, there would be significant advantages if every region, every nation, every state unit in the world didn't operate with its own money, but if as many people as possible, preferably all of them, operated with one and the same currency. Not only within an economy, but also for the world economy as a whole, the economically optimal number of currencies is one. Then the economic accounting exercised with money would function in the best possible way; the international division of labor and thus material prosperity would be supported in the best possible way.

However, this statement must be put into perspective at least in one respect: the decisive factor is *how* the single world currency comes about, who issues it. In a free market for money—in a natural process—a single world currency would emerge from the voluntary agreements of the market participants: the money demanders decide which commodity they want to use as money. It is impossible to predict with certainty what the outcome of the free choice of currency would be; after all, it resembles a discovery procedure whose outcome is not known in advance. However, it could be assumed that a commodity or precious metal currency is created, that gold is chosen as the money base, but possibly also a crypto-unit.

However, if states monopolize money production, there is no free market for money on which a single world currency could develop through voluntary decisions by people. In this case, national fiat currencies coexist for the time being. But this is not a stable equilibrium. Rather, here too, there is a tendency to create a single world currency—because, as I said, it is optimal if everyone in the world trades and calculates with the same currency. This is what democratic socialism takes advantage of.

Creating a single world currency is a means to an end for democratic socialism. Its adherents will recognize that a single world state cannot be established directly. The national resistance that would have to be overcome is still too great. The detour, the indirect way, by which democratic socialism can more easily achieve its goal, is the creation of a single world currency under state control. The eurozone can serve as a "model" for this. It has been possible here for sovereign nations to voluntarily give up their monetary sovereignty and accept a fiat single currency which is issued by a supranational central bank—which in fact can no longer be effectively controlled by the national parliaments.

The shared euro currency creates major problems in and between the participating countries. But the forced euro marriage has not yet been through the "divorce courts" because of the high costs of a euro exit and also because the democratic socialists fight any attempts to withdraw from the euro with all political means available to them. The problems created by the single currency are increasingly forcing participating countries into communization. For example, some nations must pay for the national debts of others; and the cost of saving ailing banks from collapse is borne by all taxpayers and money users.

All these problems only became apparent *after* the community of destiny was locked in—they received little or no attention beforehand. From the outset, it was not economic rationality that inspired the euro, but political endeavors that can be traced back ideologically, unsurprisingly, to democratic socialism. The end of national monetary sovereignty and the adoption of the single currency were promoted in public by emphasizing the peace and prosperity effects of euro money. The particular problems that *one* fiat money brings to many different nation-states were overlooked or ignored.

In the light of the experience gained with the "euro experiment," the question arises: *What are the consequences of creating a single fiat world currency*? Seen from a logical perspective, a pessimistic view of the future is imposed on us if democratic socialism succeeds in persuading citizens to give up their national currencies and adopt a supranational fiat currency instead. For a state-controlled compulsory world currency would bring with it all the negative characteristics and problems that any national fiat currency would, but it would cause economic, political, and cultural damage that would presumably eclipse everything that national fiat currencies do.

What every single state that has fallen victim to democratic socialism wants is also what a community of states wants: to control the production of money and to expand the money supply at will in order to secure and expand rule. It is a logical step for the states to merge their own fiat currencies into a fiat world currency—especially for small and medium-sized states, whose financial leeway is considerably increased as a result.

The fact that the choice falls on a single fiat currency and not on a commodity money is virtually self-explanatory: the national currencies are already fiat money, and fiat money is also the type of money that the states prefer for their purposes, because it can be multiplied at any time and in any quantity at the lowest cost.

If the national states agree to accept a single fiat currency, issued by a world central bank, then the money users will no longer have any choice or escape options. They will be at the mercy of fiat world money. The world central bank, which issues the fiat world currency, will not have to fear that dissatisfied users of its fiat world money will "migrate" to other currencies—because there will be no other currencies anymore. And because the single fiat world currency has no competition, it also becomes a plaything of political interests. Above all, the states will encourage the world central bank to pursue a monetary policy through which they can finance themselves as cheaply as possible by credit.

After all, debt financing is particularly attractive for every state: the possibility of easy borrowing is a very important motive for states to join a fiat world currency. Unlike with taxation, savers usually give their money voluntarily to the state, because they expect it to be repaid to them plus interest. A world central bank has a free hand to set the market interest rate as it sees fit, to set it at any desired level. It does not have to fear that capital will migrate if there is an extremely low market interest rate—after all, the same market interest rate that it determines will prevail all over the world.

A world central bank, which has the monopoly on the fiat world money, facilitates the worldwide debt economy to an extent probably unknown so far. The relatively bad state debtors, i.e., those who have so far only been able to finance themselves at relatively high interest rates, benefit in particular from a single fiat world currency. If there is only one currency left in the world, there will be a single large, transparent, and liquid world capital market in which there will no longer be any exchange rate fluctuations. This helps to reduce credit costs. The improved debt opportunities, in turn, favor the expansion of state influence. The nationalization of the economy and society is thus promoted.

The single currency will put governments in a favorable position to buy votes. The states will lure with money, and more and more citizens and entrepreneurs will become transfer recipients, beneficiaries of the state. They will benefit from state-financed jobs, social benefits, and profitable contracts. The involvement of states in economic and social life will increase. The culture of collectivism will be promoted, and individualism will be repressed. What is left of the free market economy inevitably gives way to a control and command economy in which the states play a decisive role in determining who produces what, when, and where. Although this development is also progressing under national fiat currencies, it is even more uninhibited under a global fiat currency.

With the single fiat world currency, it will be possible for the world central bank to set an artificial upswing (boom) in motion worldwide and to protect it from the downturn (bust) for a long time. Thanks to the single currency, the boom will affect all economies of the world: the prices of all labor and factor markets will be distorted by the boom—after all, there will no longer be any exchange rate movements between the economies that could shield the monetary conditions in one region from those in all other regions; all economies will thus be "monetarily aligned."

Companies and investors will continue to favor some regions of the world over others, just as investors in the eurozone see the "northern countries" as less risky than the "southern countries," and the "northern countries" will continue to be the most attractive region for investors in the eurozone. If, however, the economic developments of the participating nation-states should vary too much, the world central bank can be expected to take political countermeasures: weaker countries will be supported by it. For example, it will buy up government and bank bonds from weak countries; the many experiences of the eurozone with its "rescue policies" can serve as illustrations for this.

In this way, the world central bank can weaken or eliminate the remaining market correction forces, which could otherwise put an end to the boom. The boom it sets in motion can therefore last a long time and can also be driven a long way. However, the longer the boom lasts, the greater the damage (overconsumption and bad investments) will be. And the longer the boom progresses, the greater the costs of the correction crisis. This in turn increases the political incentives to keep the boom going by all means—after all, states shy away from recession and unemployment and the associated social and political consequences.

In order to avert the correction crisis, the states can continue to intervene in the market situation with bans and prohibitions, laws, price controls, labor and expenditure programs, and subsidy payments. Above all, however, they can now make use of the world central bank. If politically desired, it can keep any stumbling debtor afloat with newly created money and prevent the boom from crashing. This leads to the question: Will a single fiat world currency be more inflationary than national fiat currencies? The answer is yes.[112]

The primary goal that the states are pursuing with a single fiat world currency is to be able to pursue a controlled inflation policy with as little punishment as possible—with all its open and hidden redistributive effects. Controlled inflation plays into the hands of states and powerful groups whose interests are particularly closely intertwined with those of states.

However, even under a uniform fiat world currency there are limits to inflation policy. The world central bank does not have to reckon with the fact that money users will switch from the fiat world money to other currencies when inflation is high, as there are no other currencies left. But if the inflation of the fiat world currency is too high, the money users will lose confidence in it. In an extreme case (a very high inflation, a hyperinflation) people will start to escape from the fiat world money. They will no longer want to use the money, the demand for money will decline, and this could ultimately also seal the fate of fiat world money.

Of crucial importance for the inflation of the fiat world currency is which forces gain the upper hand in the decision-making body of the world

[112] Ludwig von Mises wrote clairvoyantly as early as 1912 in *Theorie des Geldes und der Umlaufsmittel*: "The single world credit bank or the world cartel of credit banks will have the power in their hands to increase the circulation of credit funds without restrictions." (Mises, *Theorie des Geldes und der Umlaufsmittel* [1912; facsimile of the first ed.; Auburn, AL: Ludwig von Mises Institute, 2007], pp. 475ff.)

central bank. In the *first case*, the governments of the states have a direct influence on the world central bank. In democracies, the rulers are known to have short-term goals: their power is only temporary. Therefore, they are anxious to maximize their current income during their term of office. Those in power do not participate in the long-term prosperity of the community, in the capital value of the economy, and consequently have no (great) interest in making decisions that maintain or increase the net present value of the community beyond their own term of office. In other words, the cow is not milked here, but slaughtered. Inflation, which the world central bank council is responsible for, will be comparatively high in this case.

In the *second case*, the council of the world central bank has decision-makers who are particularly close to the interests of banking and finance. Such a world central bank council's interest is that its "product," its fiat world currency, remains permanently marketable. It will not frivolously jeopardize the fiat world currency through implementing an exaggerated inflation policy. The world central bank council would therefore not want to slaughter the cow, but to milk it for as long as possible. This case implies that an oligarchized democracy will prevail in the world central bank council.

It is precisely then that there is a very high probability that the world central bank will above all serve the special interests to which the party oligarchs are closely linked. These are, of course, big banks and big industry (big business). The interests of the general public take a back seat and are only taken into account if they do not jeopardize the continuation of the world central bank's special-interest monetary policy: the world central bank will therefore endeavor not to let inflation become too high so that the population does not become dissatisfied and rebel against the "establishment."

Under a self-referential oligarchized democracy, in which the functionaries recruit their successors from a self-proclaimed pool, the fiat world money is even granted a particularly long stay. The democratic oligarchs will make every effort to ensure that the fiat world money system can continue to exist for as long as possible, that crises, when they occur, are effectively tackled, in such a way that the fiat world currency does not suffer, and that a "flight from money" is avoided.

In view of the over indebtedness problem that fiat money necessarily creates, we cannot exclude the idea of a *negative interest rate policy*. For example, a *negative* interest rate policy means that the central bank sets the interest rate at -4 percent per year: of a bank balance of €100.00, only €96 are left after one year, and only €66.48 euros after ten years.[113] What harms the saver benefits the debtor: he makes a profit by taking out a loan if he can borrow money at negative interest rates! Savers and investors will not tolerate this. Wishing to avoid the losses, they will go to the bank and demand that their assets be paid out in cash (notes and coins)—and the negative interest rate policy will fall on stony ground. Therefore, as long as there is cash, the effectiveness of a negative interest rate policy is limited.

However, a world central bank can easily enforce the abolition of cash by shutting down cash production. Without cash, the money is "trapped" in the accounts and can no longer be withdrawn from the banking sector. The negative interest rate policy can now be implemented unchecked. Money holders no longer have the opportunity to evade the devaluation of money and savings.[114] Individual states will welcome the abolition of cash for another reason: they will be able to track the financial dispositions of citizens and companies, which will only be able to make payments electronically at every turn: banks will be requested to provide full information on the payments and financial assets of bank customers at all times. As a result, the taxation possibilities of the states will be increased immensely.

As long as there is still cash, there are limits to taxation: if market participants feel that the tax burden is too high, they can carry out their transactions anonymously with cash. This in turn encourages states not to tax citizens and businesses too heavily. But when the taxpayers no longer have an alternative because there is no more cash, the political reluctance, which still stands in the way of increasing taxation in a world with cash, decreases. And if the financial privacy of citizens and businesses is lost, states can easily subject citizens and businesses to full monitoring.

---

[113] Who benefits from the bank customers' loss of interest? The banks debit 4 percent of customers' credit balances and transfer the money to the central bank, which then transfers the money (in the form of a profit distribution) to the state account. So it is ultimately the state and its privileged groups that earn the money from expropriating savers.

[114] An individual money holder can exchange his sight deposit for, say, company shares. However, the seller of the shares then becomes the owner of the sight deposit; it does not disappear from the monetary system.

THE DESIRE TO ABOLISH CASH

In the first half of the twentieth century, probably few people could have imagined that the US dollar and all other major currencies in the world would eventually no longer be redeemable for gold. Looking back, however, it is anything but astonishing from a logical perspective that the state has acquired a monopoly over money production and that it has also replaced the existing commodity or gold money with its own fiat money. Similarly, it can be understood that the state is seeking to abolish cash.

Cash sets limits to taxation. If people have the opportunity to carry out anonymous cash transactions, the state must exercise restraint when taxing them. If the rate of tax is too high, the market participants avoid paying it. Payments are no longer made via bank accounts, which the state can control, but with cash, which the state cannot easily track. As long as there is cash, the state must be moderate in taxation.

Therefore, cash is a thorn in the side of the state. But above all states want to get rid of it because economies are now facing an over indebtedness problem, and cash stands in the way of the "solution" they prefer. It is important to know that in the fiat money system debt grows faster than income, so that at some point debtors are crushed by credit burdens. One way of solving the over indebtedness of states and banks is through a negative interest rate policy. If the state central bank imposes a negative interest rate, debtors can reduce their debt at the expense of creditors. An interest rate of -5 percent per year, for example, reduces the value of a debt security or a bank credit of €100 to €95 in twelve months.

The savers won't put up with that. They will avoid the negative interest rate by having their bank balances paid out in cash. Cash is not devalued by a negative interest rate. As long as people have the opportunity to exchange bank balances for cash, a negative interest rate policy cannot be effectively implemented.

Cash is still very popular with many people—despite the technical innovations in payment transactions. Obviously, there are transactions where cash is preferred to electronic money. And it should not be forgotten that cash is not only in demand for payments, but also for precautionary reasons: unlike book money, which is held at banks, cash bears no risk of default. How can the state withdraw cash from circulation?

For example, by making the use of cash more expensive. Banks are encouraged to charge their customers for increased cash handling costs. Or the state can withdraw banknotes with large denominations (such as the five hundred-euro banknote). Or the state can charge maximum amounts for cash transactions. It can also devalue the cash by means of a government-fixed exchange rate for electronic book money. If the central bank charges an interest rate of -5 percent, for example, a cash withdrawal of €100 would debit the customer account €105.

As long as there is still a large number of countries in the world competing with each other for companies and talent, going it alone in abolishing cash is unlikely to be successful. A single state can do away with cash. However, the chances that it will achieve its goal in this way—by implementing a negative interest rate policy—are not too great, because those affected can switch to foreign cash. Investors' interest in a currency that is subject to a negative interest rate policy would also dwindle. Capital would be withdrawn and transferred abroad, weakening the productive forces of the economy in international competition.

The picture changes when all states move in step to withdraw cash from circulation. Money users will then no longer have any alternative options, or they will have to resort to types of money such as gold and silver or crypto units that have not previously been used on a daily basis. In order to abolish cash everywhere, however, a disciplined state cartel would have to develop. However, as has already been discussed, this is unstable. If, on the other hand, a world government with a world central bank and a fiat world currency were formed, the abolition of cash could easily be carried out.

A global central bank will claim the supervision of the banking and financial sector. It will want to prescribe how commercial banks must operate in business terms: for example, what liquidity and capital requirements they must meet and how they must assess their credit risks. The world central bank will also want to decide whether and under what circumstances failing banks will be recovered, or closed and liquidated. The right of national governments to have their say will increasingly dwindle in favor of the supranational world central bank and supranational supervisory authorities and bodies. The consequences are far reaching.

The pressure for a unification of regulation, to which all banking and financial enterprises are subject, increases—and is determined by the large and powerful interest groups. National or regional peculiarities are not taken into account if the large and powerful interest groups have asserted themselves in the political negotiation of the regulatory provisions. For many small countries, this will force far-reaching adjustments—not only in their banking and financial economies, but also in the structure of their production of goods and services. There will be winners and losers in this process: adjustment costs will be higher for some regions and lower for others. This creates conflicts of interest between the nation-states.

A fiat world currency used by people in many countries will fuel further conflicts. It is well known that the expansion of the money supply means that a few are made better off at the expense of many others: the first recipients are the beneficiaries, the late recipients the disadvantaged. This is already resulting in disputes in nation-states, which are usually characterized by a relatively homogeneous population structure in terms of culture, language, and tradition. The conflicts over redistribution become even more acute when the effects of redistribution are felt across borders: when people in one country realize that they are being bled in favor of people in another country.

A world central bank has a free hand to set the world interest rate at will. Not only can it keep it artificially low to set a boom in motion and keep it going for a long time, it can also bring about something unnatural: a negative world interest rate. One reason for pursuing a negative interest rate policy has already been mentioned: the over indebtedness problem caused by fiat world money can thus be "solved" politically. Another motive for forcing world interest rates into negative territory is the democratic socialists' desire to better steer and control the economy and society, or to shatter what is left of the free market economy.

The fact that exactly this is possible with a negative interest rate policy becomes apparent when one considers the consequences of the negative interest rate for the credit market. The commercial banks receive credit from the world central bank, say, -2 percent, on condition that they lend the money to consumers and companies. For example, if they borrow €100 at -2 percent and lend the money at, say, -1 percent, their profit is

€1.[115] Under these circumstances, however, the demand for credit would grow enormously: after all, everyone wants to profit from the negative interest rate loans.

The world central bank must ration the loans so that the creation of credit and money does not get out of hand. It is no longer the market interest rate that balances supply and demand, but the world central bank that gives a certain amount of credit and allocates it. But what criteria should be used to allocate the loans? Should all those who ask for loans get them too? Or should labor-intensive economic sectors be preferred? Or should the loans go only to sunrise industries? Or should weakening branches of industry be supported with additional loans? Or should the south get more than the north?

The world central bank has a decisive influence on who can finance and produce what, when, and where. Like a central planning authority, it—or the interest groups who control it—determines the fate of the economies in the regions of the world: which industries are promoted or pushed back; which economies grow stronger and which weaker; which banks are allowed to survive in which countries and which are not. Welcome to the centrally planned economy! However, a negative interest rate policy would not be possible in the long term; it would lead to the end of division of labor in the economy. This can be explained as follows.

First of all, lowering the interest rate inflates the prices of existing assets: stocks, houses, and land, everything becomes more expensive. The lower the interest rate, the higher the present value of future payments and thus also the market prices of the assets. The speculative bubble, which is inflated, initially provides investors with high returns. At the same time, however, the outlook for future returns deteriorates. The reason: the zero and negative interest rates cause the prices of stocks and houses, for example, to rise until the expected yield that these asset classes then promise has approached the low or negative interest rate set by the central bank. In extreme cases, the expected market returns will fall to or even below the zero line.

But once the world central bank has pushed all returns to or below the zero line, the free market economy (or what is left of it) is on the verge of collapse. Without a positive market interest rate, without the prospect

[115] By borrowing from the world central bank they gain two euros (they borrow €100 and pay back €98 after one year) and by lending they lose €1 (they borrow €1 00 and get €99 back after one year).

of a positive return, saving and investing cease: after all, every consumer and entrepreneur has a positive originary interest rate. And when there is no more return to earn, there is no more saving and investment, only consumption. The economy based on the division of labor comes to a standstill. Replacement and expansion investments fail to materialize, capital consumption begins, and the modern economy falls back into a primitive subsistence economy. The existence of billions of people would be wiped out. A horrible, extreme scenario.

The very process in which the world central bank lowers the world market interest rate to or below zero (something it can do as a monopolist of money production) is extremely problematic. It artificially pushes people's time preference up. As Friedrich Nietzsche (1844-1900) put it, there is a "revaluation of all values," a devaluation of the future. The here and now is "made" even more important than tomorrow. The consequences are far reaching. For example, life on credit is promoted. The virtue of thrift goes out of fashion. "Permanent debt" becomes morally acceptable. Achieving short-term goals becomes more important for people than achieving longer-term goals. For example, the willingness to achieve decreases, because, compared to the "disutility of labor," leisure time rises even higher in value. Divorce also becomes more attractive as a "solution" to marital problems; efforts to overcome relationship difficulties are increasingly shunned. The quality of education suffers: if the here and now is so important, then we will also spend less time on time-consuming ways of cultivating and maturing for the future. Morals decay: consideration and manners are costly activities in interpersonal relationships and often only pay off in the long term. Aesthetics degenerate: it is easy (or easier) for passing fads to find buyers; breaking away from "proven classics" is made easier. A world central bank that issues fiat money has decivilizing consequences worldwide.

The idea that states could remain sovereign and independent once they participate in the fiat world money system is illusory. If the same money is used in different countries, this will help to make the best possible use of the efficiency potential offered by the international division of labor. The commodity and factor financial markets of the national economies increasingly dovetail. And the closer the ties between them, the stronger the incentive of the nation-states to surrender sovereignty to supranational authorities. This applies both to economically good times—then the willingness to share, to make compromises is relatively high—and to economically bad times—then a way out of the economic problems is seen in moving closer together, in jointly pursued "emergency policies."

A fiat world currency promotes the political centralization tendencies within the group of states that uses it. The "urge" to establish a unified government, a world state, is strengthened, especially under the ideological leadership of democratic socialism. If economic and financial ties become ever tighter, why not create a single world state that can more effectively implement the desired policies—such as prevention of economic and financial crises as well as tax fraud, policies for environmental protection, counter terrorism, etc.—than a multitude of independent states that can only agree on and enforce their common policies, if at all, laboriously and by protracted means? The world central bank, which issues the fiat world currency, becomes a particularly sought-after political power and control center in this concentration process.

Drawing on Robert Michel's "iron law of oligarchy," it is to be expected that a relatively small, assertive group of people, which originates from the party and government structures of the participating states, will try to put the world central bank under its control and make it serviceable for its own purposes. Against this background, it would be unrealistic for something to emerge that could be described as a "democratic world central bank." The representatives of the participating states may (at least initially) endeavor to "chain" the world central bank, i.e., to design the rules and regulations to which the world central bank is subject in such a way as to prevent abuse of power.

However, what happens in the hierarchy of parties also happens in the hierarchy of a community of states: the most determined, tireless, ruthless and relentless advocates of democratic socialism prevail—above all government representatives from the participating countries, but also and above all the "experts" in the central banks and bureaucracies. The aim of the oligarchized elites will be to make the world central bank serviceable and, above all, to enable the creation of a world government, a world state, which democratic socialism must necessarily strive for.

A world state, equipped with its own fiat world money monopoly, would open a dark chapter in the history of humankind and lead to a civilizational catastrophe. It would have no more competitors to fear. No one could escape from it. Emigration would be impossible; the world state would be everywhere. The hope that the expansion of the power of the world state could be effectively curbed by democratic electoral acts would prove to be illusory as soon as an oligarchization of democracy set in—and this is to be expected, of course, as already impressively illustrated by the expansion drive of the nation-states in recent decades, and as follows from the logic of action.

It is downright absurd to think that a world state with its own fiat world currency would not sooner or later mutate into a totalitarian tyrant. One therefore does not overshoot the mark when, in the context of the dramatic consequences of a fiat world currency, one thinks of the novel *The Lord of the Rings* published in 1954 by the British writer J. R. R. Tolkien (1892–1973). In a reference to the original text, one could say:

> *One fiat world currency to rule them all, one to find them,*
> *One to bring them all and in the darkness bind them.*

But are there perhaps—as in *The Lord of the Rings*—good forces that challenge the states regarding the money monopoly and thereby effectively prevent the ideas of world money and a world state from being put into practice? One possible good force is *technological disruption*, which could revolutionize the global monetary system or show people that better money than that offered by states is both necessary and possible. There is no doubt that cryptocurrencies hold such potential for disruption. The following chapter is dedicated to this idea.

CHAPTER 21

TECHNOLOGICAL DISRUPTION: CRYPTOCURRENCIES

Bitcoin is the beginning of something great: a currency without a government, something necessary and imperative.[116]

– **NASSIM TALEB**

The crypto-unit bitcoin[117] holds out the prospect of something revolutionary: money created in the free market, money the production and use of which the state has no access to. The transactions carried out with it are anonymous; outsiders do not know who paid and who received the payment. It would be money that cannot be multiplied at will, whose quantity is finite, that knows no national borders, and that can be used unhindered worldwide. This is possible because the bitcoin is based on a special form of electronic data processing and storage: *blockchain* technology (a "distributed ledger technology," DLT), which can also be described as a decentralized account book.

Think through the consequences if such a "denationalized" form of money should actually prevail in practice. The state can no longer tax its citizens as before. It lacks information on the labor and capital incomes of citizens and enterprises and their total wealth. The only option left to the state is to tax the assets in the "real world"–such as houses, land, works of art, etc. But this is costly and expensive. It could try to levy a "poll tax": a tax in which everyone pays the same absolute tax amount–regardless of the personal circumstances of the taxpayers, such as income, wealth,

[116] "Nassim Taleb on Bitcoin: 'Bitcoin Is the Beginning of Something Great,'" Nassim Taleb (website), Mar. 23, 2013, https://nassimtaleb.org/2013/03/nassim-taleb-on-bitcoin/.

[117] It is better to speak of crypto-units, because many of the so-called crypto currencies do not yet deserve the term *currency* or *money*, because they are not very widespread, or general means of exchange.

ability, to achieve and so on. But would that be practicable? Could it be enforced? This is doubtful.

The state could also no longer simply borrow money. In a cryptocurrency world, who would give credit to the state? The state would have to justify the expectation that it would use the borrowed money productively to service its debt. But as we know, the state is not in a position to do this or is in a much worse position than private companies. So even if the state could obtain credit, it would have to pay a comparatively high interest rate, severely restricting its scope for credit financing.

In view of the financial disempowerment of the state by a cryptocurrency, the question arises: Could the state as we know it today still exist at all, could it still mobilize enough supporters and gather them behind it? After all, the fantasies of redistribution and enrichment that today drive many people as voters into the arms of political parties and ideologies would disappear into thin air. The state would no longer function as a redistribution machine; it basically would have little or no money to finance political promises. Cryptocurrencies therefore have the potential to herald the end of the state as we know it today.

The transition from the national fiat currencies to a cryptocurrency created in the free market has, above all, consequences for the existing fiat monetary system and the production and employment structure it has created. Suppose a cryptocurrency (*C*) rises in the favor of money demanders. It is increasingly in demand and therefore appreciates against the established fiat currency (*F*). If the prices of goods, calculated in *F*, remain unchanged, the holder of *C* records an increase in his purchasing power: one obtains more *F* for *C* and can purchase more goods, provided that the prices of goods, calculated in *F*, remain unchanged.

Since *C* has now appreciated compared to *F*, the prices of the goods expressed in *F* must also rise sooner or later—otherwise the holder of *C* could arbitrate by exchanging *C* for *F* and then paying the prices of the goods labeled in *F*. And because more and more people want to use *C* as money, goods prices will soon be labeled not only in *F*, but also in *C*. When money users increasingly turn away from *F* because they see *C* as the better money, the purchasing power devaluation of *F* continues. Because *F* is an unbacked currency, in extreme cases it can lose its purchasing power and become a total loss.

The decline in the purchasing power of *F* will have far-reaching consequences for the production and employment structure of the economy.

It leads to an increase in market interest rates for loans denominated in *F*.[118] Investments that have so far seemed profitable turn out to be a flop. Companies cut jobs. Debtors whose loans become due have problems obtaining follow-up loans and become insolvent. The boom provided by the fiat currencies collapses and turns into a bust. If the central banks accompany this bust with an expansion of the money supply, the exchange rate of the fiat currencies against the cryptocurrency will fall even further. The purchasing power of the sight, time, and savings deposits and bonds denominated in fiat currencies would be lost; in the event of loan defaults, creditors could only hope to be (partially) compensated by the collateral values, if any.

However, the bitcoin has not yet developed to the point where it could be a perfect substitute for the fiat currencies. For example, the performance of the bitcoin network is not yet large enough. At present, it is operating at full capacity when it processes around 360,000 payments per day. In Germany alone, however, around 75 million transfers are made in one working day! Another problem with bitcoin transactions is finality. In modern fiat cash payment systems, there is a clearly identifiable point in time at which a payment is legally and de facto completed, and from that point on the money transferred can be used immediately. However, DLT consensus techniques (such as proof of work) only allow *relative finality*, and this is undoubtedly detrimental to the money user (because blocks added to the blockchain can subsequently become invalid by resolving forks).

The transaction costs are also of great importance regarding whether the bitcoin can assert itself as a universally used means of payment. In the recent past, there have been some major fluctuations in this area: In mid-June 2019, a transaction cost about $4.10, in December 2017 it peaked at more than $37, but in the meantime for many months it had been only $0.07. In addition, the time taken to process a transaction had also fluctuated considerably at times, which may be disadvantageous from the point of view of bitcoin users in view of the emergence of instant payment for fiat cash payments.

Another important aspect is the question of the "intermediary." Bitcoin is designed to enable intermediary-free transactions between participants. But do the market participants really want intermediary-free

---

[118] Because more and more investors sell their bonds, for example. As the market supply rises, prices fall and market interest rates rise (assuming that the demand for securities remains unchanged).

money? What if there are problems? For example, if someone made a mistake and transferred one hundred bitcoins instead of one, he cannot reverse the transaction. And nobody can help him! The fact that many hold their bitcoins in trading venues and not in their private digital wallets suggests that even in a world of cryptocurrencies there is a demand for intermediaries offering services such as storage and security of private keys.

However, as soon as intermediaries come into play, the transaction chain is no longer limited to the digital world, but reaches the real world. At the interface between the digital and the real world, a trustworthy entity is required. Just think of credit transactions. They cannot be performed unseen (trustless) and anonymously. Payment defaults can happen here, and therefore the lender wants to know who the borrower is, what credit quality he has, what collateral he provides. And if the bridge is built from the digital to the real world, the crypto-money inevitably finds itself in the crosshairs of the state. However, this bridge will ultimately be necessary, because in modern economies with a division of labor, money must have the capacity for intermediation.[119]

It is safe to assume that technology will continue to make progress, that it will remove many remaining obstacles. However, it can also be expected that the state will make every effort to discourage a free market for money, for example, by reducing the competitiveness of alternative money media such as precious metals and crypto-units vis-à-vis fiat money through tax measures (such as turnover and capital gains taxes). As long as this is the case, it will be difficult even for money that is better in all other respects to assert itself.

Therefore, technical superiority alone will probably not be sufficient to help free market money—whether in the form of gold, silver, or crypto-units—achieve a breakthrough. In addition, and above all, it will be necessary for people to demand their *right to self-determination in the choice of money* or to recognize the need to make use of it. Ludwig von Mises has cited the "sound-money principle" in this context: "[T]he sound-money principle has two aspects. It is affirmative in approving the market's choice of a commonly used medium of exchange. It is negative in obstructing the government's propensity to meddle with the currency system."[120] And he continues: "It is impossible to grasp the meaning of

---

[119] See Cameron Harwick, "Cryptocurrency and the Problem of Intermediation," *Independent Review 20, no. 4 (2016): 569–88.*

[120] Mises, *The Theory of Money and Credit*, p. 414.

the idea of sound money if one does not realize that it was devised as an instrument for the protection of civil liberties against despotic inroads on the part of governments. Ideologically it belongs in the same class with political constitutions and bills of rights."[121]

These words make it clear that in order for a free market for money to become at all possible, quite a substantial change must take place in people's minds. We must turn away from democratic socialism, from all socialist-collectivist false doctrines, from their state-glorifying delusion, no longer listen to socialist appeals to envy and resentment. This can only be achieved through better insight, acceptance of better ideas and logical thinking. Admittedly, this is a difficult undertaking, but it is not hopeless. Especially since there is a logical alternative to democratic socialism: the *private law society* with a free market for money. What this means is outlined in the final chapter of this book.

[121] Ibid.

CHAPTER 22

THE RAY OF HOPE: FREE MARKET FOR MONEY AND PRIVATE LAW SOCIETY

To reverse the trend and reduce the role of government in our lives ... is a giant educational task.
— **HANS F. SENNHOLZ**

A free market for money means two things. On the one hand, those demanding money can freely choose what they want to use as money—for transaction and saving purposes. On the other hand, every market participant has the freedom to try to offer his fellow human beings a good which they want to demand voluntarily as money. But wouldn't that lead straight to "money chaos"? Wouldn't hundreds, maybe even thousands of types of money circulate and thus make financial calculation impossible in the national economy? And wouldn't that undermine the efficiency of the economy? This concern is unfounded.

The money demander plays the decisive role. In a free market for money, anyone who asks for money will, out of self-interest, ask for a good that has the greatest possible marketability, a good that is recognized by its trading partners as the generally accepted medium of exchange: money. What do you offer the baker? It is best to offer something that the baker can use to buy shoes from a cobbler or shirts from a tailor. In a free market for money, people will demand a good as money that finds the widest acceptance, that is regarded by the largest number of people as a medium of exchange. *The choice of the good that serves as money is based on the wishes of the trading partners.*

But what if Mrs. *A* offers colorfully printed paper slips and says that these are "good money"? The answer is that no one would accept her paper slips as money. Why not? Quite simple: you wouldn't know what these colorful notes are worth, or what you could get for them in exchange. That's why no one would demand them as money. This is exactly what Ludwig von Mises has shown with his regression theorem: money must arise from a good that has already had a nonmonetary market value before it can be used as money. This is not the case for colorful and arbitrarily printed paper slips. They would not be able to compete against other goods such as gold and silver.

In a free market for money, people will demand a good that possesses the physical qualities that "good money" must have. Such a good must, for example, be scarce, storable, transportable, divisible, malleable, and transferable, and it must also be regarded as valuable.[122] If we take into account the experience of currency history, it seems quite probable that money would still be chosen in the form of precious metals today—above all in the form of gold and silver. But crypto-units could also possibly assert themselves as money in the future. The choice people will ultimately make in a free market for money cannot be predicted with certainty from today's perspective.

If people opt for precious metals as money, this would be anything but a step backward compared to the unbacked fiat money. No one would have to carry jangling coins around in their pockets. The use of gold and silver can be digitalized. All kinds of payments that are common today could be carried out easily and problem-free with gold and silver. If cash is desired, precious metal coins circulate, or banknotes can be used that can be exchanged 100 percent for physical gold at the storage facility that issued the banknotes. Cashless payment transactions are also possible in the usual way when using gold money: bank transfer, direct debit, crossed check, payments by credit and debit card, mobile payment, bills of exchange, etc.

In a free market for money, two types of banks will emerge which legally will have to operate separately from each other: deposit and credit banks. *Deposit banks* offer storage, security, and payment services. For example, they provide storage capacity for physical gold and silver, protect the stored precious metals against theft, and also process cashless payments in precious metal money (settlement services). They charge their customers a fee for this. Deposit banks compete with each other for the best storage and payment services on the best terms.

[122] See J. Laurence Laughlin, *The Principles of Money* (New York: Charles Scribner's Sons, 1903), pp. 40–43.

Credit banks grant loans to credit seekers. The credit banks procure the money that is lent by issuing shares or debt securities on the capital market. For example, they offer savers interest-bearing securities in exchange for gold money. The savers transfer their purchasing power to the credit bank for the duration of the credit agreement, and the credit bank lends the money to the borrower. Although credit banks increase the volume of credit in the economy by granting credit, they do not create new money and do not distort market interest rates (as is the case in today's fiat money system).

In a free market for money, in which a good that cannot be multiplied at will (by granting credit) is chosen as money, the credit market can exercise its intended function undisturbed: the supply of and demand for savings creates a market interest rate that ensures that sufficient savings are available to make the investments. This puts an end to the chronic economic disruptions (boom and bust) caused by the issuance of fiat money. Because the banking business is not inflationary, the nonmarket (antisocial) redistributive effects of fiat money also cease.

FREE MARKET FOR MONEY—ANSWERS TO PRESSING QUESTIONS

Anyone who hears about *free market money* and *free banking* will probably pose the question: Can this work? Below are some important questions and short answers.

What happens if a deposit bank goes bankrupt? Like any company, a deposit bank can go bankrupt. However, the customer who has deposited his gold with the deposit bank does not suffer any loss: the depository bank is "only" the depository for his gold. In the event of bankruptcy, the creditors of the deposit bank have no access to the stored gold. It still belongs to the bank's customers.

Are there crises in a free market money system? Yes, there will probably also be crises in an economy where there is a free market for money. But no longer monetary crises such as the fiat money system necessarily produces.

Is there credit in a free market money system? Yes. Credit banks offer savers interest-bearing bonds. The money obtained in this way is then passed on as loans to credit seekers. However, the creation of credit by the credit banks leaves the money supply unchanged.

What happens if the money supply is so tight that goods prices fall over time? That wouldn't be a problem. The purchasing power of the money that consumers possess increases over time. It is therefore possible to reduce money holdings and demand additional goods. When commodity prices fall, companies are faced with no other challenge than rising commodity prices: their profit corresponds to the margin between turnover and costs. If prices rise, companies must ensure that their costs do not rise more than their sales; if prices fall, they must ensure that their costs decrease more than their sales.

Is there any demand for goods at all when the prices of goods fall? Yes. To explain this, let us assume that a car costs €50,000 today, and only €40,000 in a year. Those who absolutely need a car now and immediately (because, for example, their old one is broken) will buy it today. As a general rule, whether you buy now or wait to purchase depends on the *time preference*. Of course, the (marginal) benefit of buying a car for €50,000 (*U1*) is lower than of buying it for €40,000 (*U2*). In order to decide whether to buy today or in a year's time, however, the actor will compare the (marginal) utility of the purchase *today* with the (marginal) utility of the purchase *in a year's time*, discounted at his personal time preference rate (*r*, or originary interest rate). If $U1 > U2 / (1 + r)$ applies, then he buys today; and if $U1 < U2 / (1 + r)$ applies, he will wait to make his purchase. We should therefore not believe that the economy would come to a standstill if commodity prices were to fall, because nobody would buy anymore! This will not happen–if only because there are nonsuspensive needs and also because the time preference (rate) is always and everywhere positive, because time preference and originary interest can never fall to zero (let alone become negative).

What does it mean for the credit market if prices fall? There is a credit market even when commodity prices are falling. Only it would be much smaller than in today's fiat money system: debt financing becomes more expensive for the borrower–compared to credit financing in the fiat money system. At the same time, the external financing of companies by issuing new shares (in the case of stock corporations) or company member shares (in the case of partnerships) gains in importance. For old-age provision, savings would no longer be primarily in the form of debt securities, but above all in the form of money (which gains in purchasing power over time) and in the form of company shares.

Wouldn't a free banking system lead to a monopoly? In a free market for money and banks, moneyholders are free to choose the deposit bank that appears to them to be the best in comparison. New providers are always ready to attract dissatisfied customers of the deposit banks with newer and better offers. Under competitive conditions, no compulsory monopoly develops.

It is likely that in a free market for money, in addition to deposit and credit banks, other service providers will establish themselves, such as currency market and equity traders, derivatives and credit trading specialists, private equity firms, mergers and acquisitions (M&A) providers, providers of insurance services, etc., and that the market for money will also become more open. In a free market for money all kinds of modern financial and risk-hedging transactions are possible. However, the credit and financial market would be much smaller than it is in today's fiat money system. Far fewer people would work in the banking and financial sector, and labor and scarce resources would be used to a greater extent than is the case today in the production of goods.

In a free market for money, there is no central bank and no state supervisory or regulatory authorities. All that is necessary for the functioning of a free market for money is a functioning legal order which ensures that the contracting parties fulfill their obligations and that infringements of contractual agreements are effectively sanctioned: for example, that the stored commodity money is not embezzled, that banknotes can be exchanged for the money base at any time at face value. In order to guarantee this, there is no need for state monopolies of law. Jurisprudence and law enforcement can also be organized in the free market (we will return to the issue later).[123]

A free market money system—with free choice of money and bank freedom—is not a national but an international concept. If trade takes

[123] See David Dürr, "Entstaatlichung der Rechtsordnung: Ein Modell ohne staatliches Rechtsetzungs- und Gewaltmonopol," in *Individuum und Verband, Festgabe zum Schweizerischen Juristentag*, ed. Roger Zäch, Christine Breining-Kaufmann, Peter Breitschmid, Wolfgang Ernst, Paul Oberhammer, Wolfgang Portmann, and Andreas Their (Zurich: Schulthess Juristische Medien, 2006), pp. 397–414.

place internationally, across national borders, the market participants select the good to use as money with the same calculation as is used at the national level. Every user of money has an economic incentive to demand as money that good which he thinks is the most attractive means of exchange from his trading partner's point of view. The idea of a free market for money is thus global in the truest sense of the word: just as free trade knows no national borders, so a free market for money extends globally.

As the previous chapters have shown, a free market for money is incompatible with the state as we know it today, namely as a territorial compulsory monopolist with ultimate power of decision over all conflicts in its territory. There is no question that a free market for money requires far-reaching changes in people's thinking. This insight was formulated by Ludwig von Mises in 1923:

> The belief that a sound monetary system can once again be attained without making substantial changes in economic policy is a serious error. What is needed first and foremost is to renounce all inflationist fallacies. This renunciation cannot last, however, if it is not firmly grounded on a full and complete divorce of ideology from all imperialist, militarist, protectionist, statist, and socialist ideas.[124]

The state is a logical impossibility, a monstrous inconsistency: *it is a property-destroying property protector and a law-breaking law protector.*[125] But what follows from this analytical insight? Is the state in today's configuration an unavoidable evil that must be accepted inevitably and grudgingly because it is essential, because without it there can be neither justice nor security? It is tempting to answer this question in the affirmative: after all, reality shows that there are always people who disregard the property rights of their fellow human beings, who cheat, steal, rob, and murder. Honest people must protect themselves against such evildoers, and therefore law and security and their enforcement are needed. This is the only way it is possible for people to coexist peacefully and productively in the community. The conclusion is therefore that the state is indispensable.

But let's be careful not to react too hastily. If we see monkeys riding a bicycle, then we cannot conclude that *only* monkeys can ride a bicycle. If

---

[124] Ludwig von Mises, *The Cause of the Economic Crisis and Other Essays before and after the Great Depression* (Auburn, AL: Ludwig von Mises Institute, 2006), p. 44.

[125] See chapter 7.

we think that, we are subject to a logical fallacy, a *non sequitur*. If the goods law and security are in demand because they are considered necessary and indispensable, it does not mean that *only* the state can provide these goods. On the contrary, law and security can also be organized and produced in the free market—and better and more economically, by the way. Like any other good, law and security can be provided through free supply and free demand in the desired quantity and quality. *No compulsory monopoly is required for the provision of the goods law and security.*

The alternative to the state, in its present form, is the *private law society*. It is characterized by the fact that the same rules apply to all people always and everywhere: that everyone has self-ownership and that everyone has ownership of external goods acquired lawfully, i.e., non-aggressively. And since the same law applies to everyone, there is no public law apart from private law. The idea of a private law society is by no means synonymous with anarchy. Far from it! Rather, the private law society is characterized by a very clear distinction between "mine" and "yours," and violations of property are punishable and sanctioned.

It would be too far-reaching to explain in this book in detail what a private law system would look like in practice and how it would work; please refer to the bibliography for further reading.[126] At this point, however, a few brief remarks on law and security should suffice. Such mental images are helpful to better understand the idea of the free market for money.

In a private legal system, the good security is offered in the free market. On the supply side, there are insurance companies that offer security services (insurances against theft, for personal protection, etc.) in competition with other companies. In insurance contracts, the security service is specified precisely and the mutual rights and obligations are contractually laid down (such as exclusion of negligence on the part of the insured or compensation in the event of damage). The insurance contracts specify independent conciliation bodies—which also compete with each other for customers who pay voluntarily—to be called upon in the event of a dispute between the policyholder and the insurer.

[126] See for example Murray N. Rothbard, *For a New Liberty*, 2d ed. (Auburn, AL: Ludwig von Mises Institute, 2006), pp. 11, 12, and 13, 249ff.; Hoppe, *Democracy*, pp. 239ff.; Hoppe, *Der Wettbewerb der Gauner: Über das Unwesen der Demokratie und den Ausweg in die Privatrechtsgesellschaft* (Berlin: Holzinger Verlag, 2012), pp. 73ff.; also Walter Block, *The Privatization of Roads and Highways: Human and Economic Factors* (Auburn, AL: Ludwig von Mises Institute, 2009).

Under competitive conditions, it is to be expected that prices for insurance coverage, and dispute resolution will fall (while they will rise chronically in today's state-monopolized security and legal apparatus). And it is not only that the insurance services in the free market for security are more geared to the customer's demand wishes (in terms of scope and pricing); peaceableness and conflict avoidance are also promoted in this way. Those who demonstrably behave well and are friendly toward their fellow human beings, represent a smaller risk and are rewarded with comparatively low insurance premiums.

Since an insurance company is contractually obliged to indemnify the policyholder in the event of a loss (e.g., in the event of a burglary), it will take a great deal of effort to prevent the occurrence of a loss. And if the damage has nevertheless occurred, the insurance company will do everything in its power to track down the perpetrator and make him liable; otherwise, it will have to pay the compensation, which in turn will reduce its profit. The free market for security discourages crime, because potential perpetrators face highly efficient private insurance providers and police agencies. Such insurance and legal contracts can be established not only nationally, but of course also internationally, for private households as well as companies.

In a private law society, a free market for money is a natural phenomenon in the truest sense of the word: a free market for money is the logical consequence of people's right to self-determination when choosing money. The voluntary agreement of the people involved in the global division of labor would (presumably very quickly) result in a single world currency. A freely chosen world currency differs categorically from a single fiat world currency, which is the passion of the democratic socialists. A world currency chosen in the free market for money would literally be economically and ethically good money, which best serves humankind, which best promotes a peaceful and cooperative coexistence of people in this world.

EPILOGUE

A BETTER WORLD IS POSSIBLE

In a word, the progress of a science is blocked because erroneous methodological principles prevail.
— **CARL MENGER**

The development of humankind is not preprogramed. It does not follow a predetermined path, as Karl Marx and Friedrich Engels wanted their readers to believe. It is rather the ideas (or theories) that guide people's actions; this is a statement that is logical, a statement that cannot be refuted by logical means. And because it is true, it also explains why all those who strive for power over their fellow men and women—be they feudal lords, kings, emperors, tsars, dictators, democratic government representatives, or oligarchs—want to gain sovereignty over ideas: the one who determines which ideas are considered true and right and which do not possesses true power over his fellow human beings.

Today, above all, it is the state that has a particular power of influence over opinion, and in this way, it tries to expand its position of power. Meanwhile, most people do not take offence at it anymore. For them, the state is something good: it is an employer, educator, lawyer, judge, patron, environmentalist, reliable debtor, punctual pension payer, guarantor of stable money and sufficient credit, fighter against injustice and guardian of fair pay, patron of health and old-age provision, and much more. Yes, for many people the state can no longer be imagined without what is generally regarded as a "good life."

Democratic socialism, as the dominant ideology of the modern state, has done a thorough job. It has not only reshaped the spectrum of people's opinions and values, but it has also clouded the imagination of many people. Who still thinks today that most people and their families, their friends, their community, and their fellow citizens would be much better off if the state did *not* exist? That without this state there would be fewer economic crises and wars in the world? Probably very few. Many people also do not understand where the unthinking acceptance of the state actually leads: into bondage, into serfdom.

The fact that this logical consequence of the state's actions can largely be concealed to this day is primarily due to one cause: the social and economic sciences are at war with a priori theory. That is because, in order to gain knowledge, they follow the scientific method. They formulate hypotheses (conditional statements, "If A, then B") and then test their truth content on the basis of observational data. This, however, is a procedure that for a number of reasons cannot be applied meaningfully in the social and economic sciences and that furthermore politicizes and corrupts the social and economic sciences.

The scientific method, which in recent decades has been applied more and more strongly and uninhibitedly in economics, has cultivated skepticism and relativism—according to principles such as: "There is no truth, everything can be doubted" and "All knowledge is only relative, never universally true." This has contributed to the a priori rejection of knowledge in today's social and economic sciences: they ignore or reject the insight that there are irrevocable laws in the field of human action that can be fathomed and justified by logical thinking.

From the point of view of social scientists and economists, the economy and society have thus been degraded to something like an experimental laboratory or field of experimentation. No matter how peculiar theories may be, people can still claim, with reference to universally accepted science, that the truth of these theories can ultimately only be established by trial and error, by a practical test. And if a theory sounds politically promising, they will want to put it into practice—and no sociologists and economists will be able to raise serious objections to it unless they want to be labeled unscientific, antiprogressive and narrow-minded.

It is not surprising that political forces use the opportunity to harness social and economic science for their own purposes. Above all, political parties and governments use taxpayers' money to promote and pay for those scientists who formulate and disseminate politically acceptable theories and who demand a practical test for their theory with reference to well-founded science. It is not surprising that the state, as a source of work and income for science, is adulated, idealized, and glorified by privileged scientists. However, the problem addressed by this is actually much bigger, as Murray N. Rothbard made clear:

> [S]ince the early origins of the State, its rulers have always turned, as a necessary bolster to their rule, to an alliance with society's class of intellectuals. The masses do not create their own abstract ideas, or indeed think through these ideas independently; they follow passively the ideas adopted and promulgated by the body of intellectuals, who become the effective "opinion moulders" in society. And since it is precisely a moulding of opinion on behalf of the rulers that the State almost desperately needs, this forms a firm basis for the age-old alliance of the intellectuals and the ruling classes of the State. The alliance is based on a quid pro quo: on the one hand, the intellectuals spread among the masses the idea that the State and its rulers are wise, good, sometimes divine, and at the very least inevitable and better than any conceivable alternatives. In return for this panoply of ideology, the State incorporates the intellectuals as part of the ruling elite, granting them power, status, prestige, and material security. Furthermore, intellectuals are needed to staff the bureaucracy and to "plan" the economy and society.[127]

A world currency and a world state, which were discussed in the previous chapters, are only possible through ideas that are regarded by the public as right and good. Therefore, in order for the hope for a better world to be justified, in order for the way not to lead into a world state via a world currency, enlightenment is necessary—just as Immanuel Kant once formulated it:

> Enlightenment is man's emergence from his self-inflicted immaturity. Immaturity is the inability to use one's mind without another's guidance. This immaturity is self-inflicted if the cause of it lies not in the lack of understanding, but in the resolution and courage to make use of it without another's guidance. Sapere aude! Have courage to use your own mind! is the motto of the Enlightenment.[128]

Applied to economics, Kant's enlightenment concept can be put into practice as follows: *with unbiased logical thinking, we come to the conclusion that economics is not an empirical science, but an a priori*

---

[127] Rothbard, *For a New Liberty*, p. 67.

[128] Immanuel Kant, "Beantwortung der Frage: Was ist Aufklärung?," *Berlinische Monatsschrift*, 1783, p. 516.

science of action.[129] Economics does not gain its theories through "testing," but through strict action-logical thinking. And strict action-logical thinking is also the testing authority that is able to conclusively judge the correctness or falsity of theory; experience cannot do that.

Understanding and practicing economics in this way will destroy the foundations of the driving force of democratic socialism, which for decades has been working toward establishing a world state with its own world currency and has already made considerable progress along this path. The reference to bad experiences, undesirable developments, and crises will not be able to deprive democratic socialism of its power and overcome it. This can only be achieved by insight into the better ideas, by the struggle of arguments of reason. This book is meant as a contribution to help the better ideas prevail.

[129] For an overview of the arguments see Thorsten Polleit, "Kritik der ökonomischen Erkenntnis," *Ludwig von Mises Institut Deutschland, Feb. 22, 2019, https://www.misesde.org/2019/02/kritik-der-oekonomischen-erkenntnis/.*

APPENDIX

ON THE LINK BETWEEN THE A PRIORI CATEGORIES OF ACTION AND REALITY

This short appendix aims to address an important issue: How is it possible that the a priori categories of human action derived from human cognitive faculties (mind or spirit) coincide with the real world? In other words, how can the categories of human action provide insights into the real world? After all, they are only insights into the human mind itself.[130] Why do things in experienced reality, for example, obey the cause-and-effect relationship (causality) when that is a category designed by the human mind? Is it not necessary to conclude that the human mind creates reality, and would that not be a rather questionable idealistic assumption?

One possible answer to these important questions can be developed as follows: The a priori categories of action are derived from the human cognitive faculty. Human action is undoubtedly bound to physicality, to human physical existence in the real world. Human action is, so to speak, always and everywhere physically or bodily; one can also speak of the a priori of corporeality. For example, if you say something, you have to make your vocal cords vibrate; if you walk from here to there, you have to use your legs; if you think, you have to let your brain work.

The a priori categories of action of the actor, his spirit and his mind, have an essential connection with the physical world via physicality or corporeality: the categories of action logic that claim to provide knowledge about the real world (like the sentence "Humans act") follow from the interaction of the physical corporeality of the actor (*Körperlichkeit*) with the real world.[131] The categories of action are thus not only mental, spiritual states, but they are at the same time always connected with the qualities of the real world in which action is taken; they can be traced back to them.

[130] On this point, see Hans-Hermann Hoppe, *Economic Science and the Austrian Method* (Auburn, AL: Ludwig von Mises Institute, 2007), pp. 17–22.

[131] See Höffe, *Immanuel Kant*, p. 43, who uses this phrase; see also Peter Janich, who points out that one mostly speaks of the body (*Körper*) when actually corpus (*Leib*) is meant: "The difference is easy to point out: a part of a body is also a body; a part of a corpus (*Leib, TP*) is not itself a body, because it is not viable if it is separated." (Janich, *Handwerk und Mundwerk: Über das Herstellen von Wissen* [Munich: C. H. Beck, 2015], p. 227).

What needs to be clarified now is how the interaction of the actor with the physical world produces a cognitive faculty useful for the real world. Ludwig von Mises offers a theoretical evolutionary explanation: The mind categories have developed over the course of evolution.[132] Those people who were successful were those whose minds were able to correctly grasp, interpret and respond to the real world. Their characteristics prevailed in evolution. Those who were unable to do so perished. We can therefore speak of a feedback process that has taken place between the mind of the actor and the real world: the a priori categories of action that the actor has at his disposal determine the view, the perception of the real world. And the real world determines, namely through the successes and failures of action, the conditions under which the actor perceives and looks at the real world.

The doctrine of human action, based on the undeniably true statement that humans act, opens up the possibility of effectively countering the fundamental and stubborn criticism of idealism (as the antithesis to realism) and above all of Immanuel Kant's "transcendental idealism." This criticism is roughly as follows: the denial of a subject-independent world is untenable, and Kant's transcendental idealism is contradictory. Idealism means that reality, as perceived by the actor, is nothing other than the content of human acts, that reality is exclusively a human-cognitive product. Realism, on the other hand, believes that the real world, its concrete existence, is independent of the mental states of those acting.

Immanuel Kant, however, is not an idealist in the sense mentioned above. A concluding attempt will be made to justify this statement. Kant argues that there is the "thing in itself" (he speaks of "noumenon": the imagined thing, the ideas of nonexperienceable objects) as opposed to an appearance (which he calls the "phenomenon"). According to Kant, we experience things as our cognitive faculty makes them appear to us, and from them the mind forms insights. We attribute qualities to the things of the real world that we experience, qualities that go back to exercising our cognitive faculty.

A central thought in Kant's "Critique of Pure Reason" is that our insight is not directed toward the objects of the real world, but the objects of experience are directed toward our capacity for insight. For example, time and space are not characteristics that "things in themselves" have, but they are "pure forms of perception;" they go back to the exercise of our cognitive faculty: the human cognitive faculty perceives things in space and time.

---

[132] See also Mises, *Nationalökonomie*, pp. 36ff.

Now, it seems to be idealistic to say that things are not really as they are experienced by us, but that we experience things only as our cognitive faculty allows–and Kant argues this way. But he combines this view with an important insight. It is this: the fact that we do not experience things as they really are, but only as they appear to us, opens the possibility that there are true synthetic judgments a priori about the objects of experience.

The question in Kant's transcendental philosophy is: How are synthetic judgments possible a priori? The answer is as follows: if an object without the condition *F*, which in turn is based on the exercise of our human cognitive faculty, can never be the content of an objectifiable insight of experience, then the statement "All objects of experience necessarily fulfill the condition *F*" is a synthetic judgment a priori. The principle of transcendental philosophy is: "Conditions of the possibility of objective experience, which derive from our cognitive faculty and its exercise, are conditions of the experienced objects themselves and are a priori asserted by these objects in synthetic judgments."[133]

If one agrees up to this point, then the sentence "Humans act" can be understood as a synthetic judgment a priori in the Kantian sense: No objectified experience can be made that could contradict the sentence "Humans act" and the categories it contains. All experience about human action is bound to the (praxeo)logical categories of action; it is only possible through its application. And as shown above, no idealistic assumption is required to show that the phrase "Humans act" and the categories it contains (as pure concepts of understanding) provide true knowledge about the physical world.

Let us conclude with Ludwig von Mises: The "real thing" with which praxeology has to do is human action, that shares a root with human reason. That reason is able to fathom the essence of action through mere thought is due to the origin of action from reason. The propositions of praxeology obtained through consistent and error-free thinking are not only completely certain and indisputable like the propositions of mathematics; they refer with all their certainty and indisputability to action as it is practiced in life and in reality. Praxeology therefore conveys exact knowledge of real things.[134]

---

[133] Tetens, *Kants "Kritik der reinen Vernunft,"* p. 113.
[134] Mises, *Nationalökonomie*, p. 20.

INDEX

Compiled by Roger E. Bissell

ABOUT THE AUTHOR

Thorsten Polleit, born 1967, has been Chief Economist of Degussa, Europe's largest precious metals trading company, since April 2012. Prior to this, he worked for fifteen years in international investment banking. From 2014 to 2018 he was honorary professor of economics at the University of Bayreuth. Thorsten Polleit was awarded the O.P. Alford III Prize in Libertarian Scholarship. He is adjunct scholar at the Ludwig von Mises Institute, Auburn, Alabama, USA, and president of the Ludwig von Mises Institut Deutschland. Thorsten Polleit is a co-founder of an Alternative Investment Fund (AIF).

His personal website is: www.thorsten-polleit.com.

Made in United States
North Haven, CT
29 April 2023

36024905R00104